NEVER GIVE UP

NEVER GIVE UP

DIVYA G PRASAD

NU VOICE
PRESS

NU VOICE PRESS

First published by NU VOICE PRESS 2024
An imprint of Hubhawks Pvt. Ltd
www.nuvoicepress.com

ISBN: 978-81-966888-9-9

Typeset by Saanvi Graphics, Noida
Printed at Thomson Press
Published by Nu Voice Press

Author's Note

(The Pledge)

There is always "A WAY" to a problem and then there is "AWAY" from a problem. Which one would you choose?

Dear reader,

It is not even a choice. Not even if you are going through depression. Life is all but phases of schooling, a constant loop of learning and failing. Our goal is to never stop learning and rise to a fall.

All survivors have one dictionary of words in common. It is to better us every day and to live for the people who matter to us and vice-versa. Live to inspire others.

These stories are just eleven. The stories have hit people of any age. The stories have not investigated a caste. The stories are not biased on any gender. The stories, oblivious to another person, near and unknown to us, are of sailing in the same boat. They are not just stories. The book is a small province of a large rogue called depression.

Mental sickness is real. I constantly carry a pill. Sometimes an anti-depressant, sometimes for anxiety, I have a pill for all my moods. Happy or sad, I need them. The pill's name is "FRIENDS". They are freely available in all walks of life. They never run out of stock. You just need to preserve them carefully.

Our own life's film is a blend of a hero and a villain that resides within us. With depression, there is always one of these overpowering the other. Hence, the need to talk about it. Nurture the angel within you and kill the growing demon.

Life is like a fictional novel.
Each page a twisted throttle.
Some pages sad, a lot happy.
Never ever giving up half-way.
As you progressed to the finale,
Stumbling towards darkness but rising to the valleys,
It provides a sweet closure,
Carrying a story, a one of your own, in full measure.
Once your novel is completed and shelved,
Your life's purpose comes to a full circle.
A new novel, then awaits your story to be told.

Pledge yourself to this life's giving's. Behold the struggle, for it is temporary. What is permanent, is the willingness to strengthen yourself.

NEVER GIVE UP.

CHAPTER 1

The Office

I knew what grieving was. I lived through it for a part of my life. Now, it felt like a large piece of my cake was being snatched away while I stood in silence, as I knew it was meant to be eaten by someone else. The grieving came back like a thunderstorm. Cakes did not last long, did they? But, while they were at their tasty best, they gave the content one was hoping for, making the heart lighter with each piece that stuck between our teeth. My life with dad was similar. I called him Pappa. And today, his end had dawned, he had left for worlds unknown to the mortal beings. Just like with the cake, I did not feel content with the time I spent with Pappa, and neither did my heart feel light.

The rituals were far more painful than the grieving itself. I was tired from all the crying, consoling, and committing to the rituals diligently. What was even more tiring was to tell my mind and heart that Pappa was no more with us. It took me time. It really did.

"Move on," people advised. I wondered what it meant. Time heals, they said. Only later did I realise the real meaning of "move on".

We cannot leave the past while being in the present. What we leave are just our physical footprints behind, but we take a lot of memories and life lessons forward so that the past tunes our future. What we tell ourselves in the present, when we say, "move on" is just that the past was not as promising as we expected, but we can still carve out a beautiful future. Time makes it better and acceptable.

With mom leaving us at a noticeably young age, Pappa donned all possible roles. Being a strict mother and an understanding dad was not easy, at least according to me. It did not show on his face though. Often, he cried in the solitude of his room, looking at mom's photo. I was not a troublesome child, he said. Nevertheless, I was still a helpless child, and it meant pushing a bit harder to get through the day.

Men have never been trained to juggle between a profession and being a homemaker. Pappa learned a few cooking hacks from relatives. He browsed through YouTube videos that read, "Instant recipes". One of my aunties had suggested that he hire a cook.

He rejected it saying, "There is nothing more beautiful to come home from work and cook a nicely-laid dinner for the family. The small talks we had have been a large portion of my memories. Microwave-heated food is not to be served during those conversations."

Some of his friends advised him to re-marry because I needed a mother at that tender age.

He rubbished those theories too: "My wife and I were married, once and for all of our lifetime. With her gone, our 'forever' has not yet died. My happiness knew no bounds when I held my child in my arms for the first time. And how will I let this little happiness be placed into somebody else's hands? She can be his mother and hopefully a good friend too. But he will always be mine and only mine."

Pappa had sailed through each day like a droplet of an ocean, just going with the flow. Most probably because his mind was trained for it. Most probably because of his profession. Pappa was a therapist. A passionate one.

He used to often quote himself, "Being a therapist doesn't mean our patients have to be mad. Sometimes people just need an extra, unbiased listener to their sorrows rather than one who is always suggesting you to overcome it. I am that listener. What's more important than listening is also to question them about certain things that will trigger their thought process and eventually would lead them to think what is right for them rather than dwelling on what is going wrong with them."

I often thought of his profession as an unlikely breadwinner. Like, how many of us have problems so big that we need a third party to verify the same?

Pappa had continued the argument, "I am not stamping anything for them. For an eye that sees them from afar, their suffering is microscopic. But for the one who is already in turmoil, the problems seem like a hard rock pressed against their head."

I had commanded, "Dad, problems or not, that madhouse is not where you should be spending time now. It is time for you to retire. You have done your duties well, and now, let me serve you."

I had always believed that no problems are big unless we make them big. Pappa never let me serve him, not even once. He breathed his last while on the job, listening to people's non-existent problems.

Finally, I got to shut down the madhouse now. Even though his office was attached to the left of our home, I never once visited it. I did not know what the interiors held. Probably a lot of emotions stuck on the walls that roared for help, and amidst all this chaos would be my calm Pappa, cleaning all their stained feelings, feeding them with the right choices in life. For the first time in my thirty years, I unlocked the office, to let me in the world of Pappa.

As I entered, I let the atmosphere sink in. The office was not sulking at all. Scanning it from left to right, I took careful steps. The doormat said to leave the footwear outside. In quick succession, I retraced my steps back, removed my shoes, and stepped in again, barefoot. I have always gone to a hospital or clinic with my shoes on! The only places I could think of taking them off were either temples or our own home. This was neither of those! Then why remove my shoes?

Office, for me, had chairs, desks, a wardrobe of files, and all things a traditional clinic looked like. I had stepped into something different. It was not like an office, but more like a home! And that explains why shoes were made to not enter. A large blue sofa sat in one corner of the room. The bright yellow curtains patterned the entrance of sunlight. There were study books on the sky-high shelf, probably from Pappa's college days. Not only study books, he had a few novels by famous writers too. The patient files were stacked in perfect unison on one of the smaller shelves. A large, peacock-embroidered carpet slept in the middle of the room. The left-out space was occupied by white marble flooring that gave a soothing feeling to the toes. A sense of calmness already welcomed you. My nose had already cautioned me of disinfectant smells present in a clinic. Here again, my nose survived. An *agarbathi* essence smoked the room. Maybe the house-help lit it every day for Pappa. I did not see any kind of medicines anywhere or even any medical instruments for the treatment of patients. My knowledge about Pappa's profession was limited.

I called them patients, for obviously they were someone who needed treatment. Pappa differed though. He always called them by one name: Hope. I never knew why and did not intend to argue about it either. I sat comfortably on the sofa, wondering what I should do next. This place did need cleaning. A few books bore the "long long ago" look. Dust settled on most items in the room. What I had not failed to notice, though, was a table far away, opposite the sofa, sparkling, as if the dust pretended it was not even there, was our family photo. Pappa, Mamma, and a little me. The mere look of it sent me gushing waters down my eyes again. I walked up to the table, sobbing, and steadily held the photo against my heart. I had not once checked on his work life.

I took a deep breath, heaved a light sigh, and concentrated on the place again. I would always wonder what kind of "Hope" visited Pappa. So, I decided, that the first clean-up of this home should start from his Hope files. There were many, and I did not have the interest to read every one of them. I had no interest in books. Reading somebody's story was way out of my league. But, to let the curiosity cat out of my head, maybe I will look for a name, a label, or the purpose of their visits and start reading their hurts. Just as that thought struck me, I saw a pile of eleven files under a desk where my family stood. Pappa was probably working on them recently. I picked up the files. I had to sit at home and think this through as to how to dispose this madhouse, after, of course, a little bit of cleaning. For now, the eleven files can give me company. I locked the door with sadness glooming all over me again. When I walked to the gate, I shot one look at the Hope-home again as if Pappa had called my name. Realising my foolishness, I walked away to my home with the eleven files, hugging them to my chest. Strangely, something breezed past me, infusing cooler and calmer emotions inside my heart. It felt light. A small piece of the cake lay in my hand, ready to be eaten.

CHAPTER 2

The Hope Notes

The last few days of Pappa's life clouded my mind. The things he did, the things he said, and the things he wanted me to do. Pappa kept pressing on one point most of the time, "I hope the hopes are doing okay; I am proud of all of them equally." I would laugh it off as it sounded funny.

I would ask him, "What kind of poem are you building? Any new hobby, Pappa?"

Pappa would stare me in the eyes and with a lot of expectation from me, would request, "Son, promise me that you will read the Hope files once."

Brushing it off, I said, "That's never going to happen in your lifetime!" I cried profusely at this conversation we had, and to think of it, that was Pappa's last wish. I vowed to uncover the stories that these Hope files held. To help me prioritise which stories to read first, I wanted to know the gist of them. And I hoped that would be the first page in each file. Hopefully, a symptom, purpose of visit, name, and such details were what a first finding should offer. I was wrong. I know why the files felt light. Because they literally had nothing in it to offer my impatient brain.

I opened the first file. My expression traversed at lightning speed from expectation to disappointment to shock to confusion. There was nothing but a single paper. The heading of the page said, "Towards Hope." I flipped the paper two to three times, making sure some text would exhibit the actual note. Nothing. At the centre of the paper, was written, boldly, in cursive handwriting, the following text—

NEVER GIVE UP

A

I second-guessed what the other files might hold too. Anyway, to confirm my theory, hurriedly, I opened all the eleven files. I placed all of them on the floor, opened, facing me. All of them read the same. Ok, this was getting really mysterious. Firstly, why did Pappa possess notes, even though they were blank? Secondly, what did these decipher to? I scratched my chin. With legs pressed against my chest, I sat with the files, just as blank as they were. Wasn't anything happening with these patients? Why are they empty? Just then, I noticed a teeny date at the bottom-right corner of the paper. It read, "Hope date" and the date. Every small detail on the paper was throwing me off. Pappa loved riddles and he used them in his files too? Wow. At least he could have thought of the person reading this in future. Specifically, me. How could I decipher these? It was way out of my league. Not giving up, I flipped each of the files again, twice, to spot any other hint. Nothing. What did the text mean? What did the date mean? What were these references to "Hope"? Hope I find out. *Ufff*, this "Hope" word has stuck with me now. Anyway, I am never giving up, as Pappa would always tell me. Yes, the files have decided that I am going towards them with a hope to uncover the secret they hold.

Priya's call got me out of the daze. I was once again thankful to her, like many other times. In quick succession, I shut the haunting faces of the files.

I should be concentrating on Priya and myself. We were to wed in two months. A lot of wedding formalities had to be accomplished. That burden though did not seem to hamper my days as Priya was by my side, attending to the smallest of the desires. We decided to go ahead with the wedding after consultation with the priests.

I cut a sorry face, as I opened the front door.

"What have you been doing?" Priya shouted. "My hands are paining just from ringing the bell N number of times! Ultimately, I decided to call on your phone. Seriously, what have you been doing? The toilet also does not entertain you for thirty minutes."

I pinched her cheeks and let out a quick laugh. "I am sorry. I was cleaning up some stuff of Pappa. Forget that. What got you in here so early in the morning? Already missing me?"

"You wish!" she chided. "Pappa was reluctant to push the wedding dates, even on his deathbed. Pappa was much more thoughtful with our wedding than we ourselves are. He prepared everything well for our union as well as his departure without causing any hindrance. We have two months. You don't have to worry. I will call whenever I need your help. We do not want to disappoint Pappa. Would we? Not me, for heaven's sake. I am his pride. I was his favourite, and you know that. So, I am getting you on board for everything now. Are you ready?"

With a stern salute, I answered, "Aye-Aye Captain! Where do we start?"

Priya banged a blank paper on the table.

"What is this?" I enquired.

"Firstly, we need to list out things that need our immediate attention. Then we call our wedding planners for the designs of the hall. Then we call up the cooks. Then we must plan for out-station guests. Then we must book their flights. Then we must print out a photo of Pappa." She was letting out her mind too fast. Just before she got to her next "then", I cut her short.

"Wait, too much information for my brain to process. First things first. The list that needs immediate attention. Okay?"

She smiled and nodded her head in agreement. Priya was still smiling.

I asked her, "What is your train of thought called?"

Confused, she asked, "What? What do you mean?" I could bet on the face she would show next.

"Well, have you ever thought of naming your train of thoughts? Maybe Rajdhani? Because it runs non-stop just like your mouth!" The face came. Angry. Next, an unpredictable question.

"My dear, you missed a party with your friends so you could catch this train. Didn't you?"

"You knew?" I asked, surprised.

"Pappa told me. I told you I was his favourite." Priya had the last word.

Pappa had introduced me to her. I was just stepping out with my friends that day. The usual weekly meet, when Pappa had gotten her home. I briefly said hi and without waiting for her reply, I immediately added, "Bye Pappa," and turned towards the door. She probably thought I was lacking in basic manners. The truth was, I hardly cared for anybody, except my friends, of course, and Pappa, to behave properly. Destiny had penned something else, and who knew she would be one of the few to receive my care, in near future.

Pappa stopped me right when I stepped on the doormat. Without reprimanding me, he asked, "Why don't you prepare some freshly-brewed coffee for us? I am sure Priya would be spellbound by your coffee."

As they walked towards the sofa, he went on to brag about me for quite some time. Even though proudness clouded me for the happiness I had gifted Pappa, it was unsettling for me to hear it in front of a total stranger. I was in the kitchen, preparing the supreme coffee as hinted by Pappa. The moment Pappa stopped talking and gave way for Priya to speak, I fell in love. As I mixed my special coffee, the love was brewing inside me with every word she spoke. Her intellectuality and superior voice flattered each other. She had me floored by the time the coffee was piping hot. I felt like that shy girl who wanted to impress her prospective groom with a coffee. I handed them their cups of coffee and placed myself comfortably on a sofa opposite her.

She sipped the coffee in between her conversations. I was lost by then. I skipped the meeting with my friends. Her beauty went past that which a normal eye could see. Her words sounded like lip-syncs now, the sound blurred. And I loved this feeling for the first time. A time when someone had really touched my heart, not physically yet. I sat on the sofa, stone-like, occasionally swinging my head to see both. I sat hypnotised by those beautiful eyes.

"Didn't you need to join your friends for the weekly meet?" Pappa questioned me after a while.

"Well, that meeting got cancelled. I will be here if you guys need anything. Please carry on," I replied.

Both of them looked at each other and laughed hard. Sheepishly, I laughed too for no reason. They continued their conversation and I still had placed my bum on the sofa and eyes on her. I do not know for how many minutes or maybe hours she sat there, chatting with Pappa. I had not spoken a single word. I brought myself back from that realm when Priya got up to take our leave. I wished she stayed for some more time. That "some more time" being a lifetime.

As I waved her a bye, not literally, but as a courtesy, Pappa smiled and patted on my shoulder.

"You cancelled the meet. Didn't you?" I hugged him tight in response. He had played cupid perfectly.

With some caution, I explained my feelings to Pappa. I could not take her out of my mind. I was literally being mechanical at the office. I was a regular at the coffee café now, cherishing my coffee even more. Pappa's elation could not be measured because he confessed later that he had set this up for me. Pappa knew Priya was the one for me. When he invited her home, she knew this was her future home. They only needed me to be on the same page.

Now that I was, the dates were set. My home smelled of a wonderful future. We did want more time to know each other and that was why we planned for the wedding after a year. The engagement was done with much grandeur.

It is true that when God gives us a bundle of happiness, he takes away some part of it in return. And that return had come in the form of Pappa's death. All I was left with in this earthly being now was Priya.

The home still smelled of a wonderful future. And I thanked Pappa for handing Priya to me. And I thanked Priya for her entrance into my life, like I thanked her many other times.

Our high-level ticks were done on the list. Most of the items were already taken care of. I had Priya's time now before she went on to call our wedding planners.

"Care for a cup of coffee?" I asked.

"Sure, chef!" She answered.

I went off to the kitchen. I rehearsed my dialogues. I had to confide my inner Tsunamis to Priya. The files were bothering me.

I searched for Priya in the living room. Had she left? I gave a quick round of the room.

She called out from the study room, "What are these files?"

I told her of my visit to Pappa's office and the finding of the files. I should say that I was well-rehearsed. I was able to convey my feelings perfectly or maybe it was Priya. She was an understanding person. When love happens, the feelings communicate more through the eyes rather than words.

Priya held my palm. "Pappa would have never wanted you to find these. Now that you have, I know for sure you will be hell-bent on researching. Take your time. Do not worry. I will do my best to take care of the wedding preparations."

Confused, I asked, "But why? There is nothing in these files anyway. I just wanted you to know of this and get it off my chest."

Priya quietened me. "I already know. Why do you keep forgetting that I was Pappa's favourite?"

"Then tell me what this is all about," I said, irritated.

Priya packed the list in her bag. She hugged me. She stood close to the front door. All this while I was just glaring with confused looks.

Before she closed the door, she answered, "You need to find out. And you better. We have sufficient time for our big day! Do not worry. I am going to take care of all the work for the wedding. And you will be closing these files before the big day. Done deal?"

In my mind, I whispered, "Aye-Aye Captain."

Later that day, in office, I looked at my computer screen, trying to type, but something in my mind skipped that professional thinking. While I was there physically, mentally I was strewn all over the place. This was not like the time I was in love. Priya had made me like this when we were in the first few days of our courtship. She occupied a great deal of my mind, along with my heart too. Today was different. A nagging insect was eating me. It chose not to let go of me until I went to Pappa's office again.

The files flashed in front of my eyes from time to time as I waved them off constantly. Getting no work done today, I excused myself from office. The excuse was lame.

"Boss, I would like to take a few days of leave even before my planned leave for my wedding. I still need to shake off my Pappa's death," I said to my Manager while thinking of myself.

I was not sure if I had hit him with the marriage card or Pappa's death. It worked and he gave me fifteen more days of leave.

Little did he know that neither of these was my motive. I could not sleep until I unwrap the Hope stories, which is strange for a non-reader like me. I needed to get to the bottom of this. And if that means, hunting down these people, potentially suicidal, so be it. I had eleven files. I intended to venture one file, one day. And so, the extra leaves, until my wedding day.

I did not want Priya to be missing out on this action. Priya being Priya, was all supportive. I did not want to carry the weight (even though there was none) of these files to the wedding day or beyond it.

This had to be done with right now. Starting today.

While the heart is undergoing a lot of emotions, the otherwise serene mind also fails to provide clarity of thought. Today, on the first day of my leave, zealous as ever before, I opened the door to the office again. I went straight to the sofa, sinking down my butt and so did my mind. For a few minutes, I gathered all things around, expressionless. *Just give me one hint.* I could start from there. Hope.

I did not want to give up just yet. With closer, suspicious looks that covered my otherwise dull face, I rescanned the entire shelf. That is it. There, I found it. Boldly gawking at me, the shelf that probably mocked me for not finding it in the first place. Written on it were just the words I was looking for: The Never Gave Up files.

Alright, the first step was done. Now, I need to hover over each of these stories and really find out the truth! I will finally get a suitable answer to the burning question inside me: why did Pappa possess these blank notes? Yes, I will get the names now, and the reason why they had thought life wasn't on their side.

Here is where I underestimated Pappa. From an early age, Pappa was an avid reader. He loved listening to stories, real or fiction. He would hardly get through ten pages per day of a book. That was his way of dwelling on each character and their emotions. That was his sheer determination to pursue his therapist journey. He loved to read people's minds, listen to them and just soak in their stories. And as in every book, trying to come out of that part of the story, to close one book, whether happy or sad and to continue life with a fresh start of carving another story. I was the one who did not like stories. How many ever times Pappa tried to pester me, I would excuse myself.

And now, what was I to become? An avid reader. But let us just keep it to these files. I could not go more than a hundred pages. So, this fifteen days, one file, one day. Kudos to that reader inside me, hopefully Pappa has passed on some genes regarding this.

I keyed the door. Feeling happy. Smiling. The files touched against the side of my heart. Did that breeze hit me again? Yes, it did indeed. This time though, my heart felt heavy and so did the weight of the files. The cake was about to get out of my hands again!

I placed all the files on the floor to visualise my reading pattern. Looking at them, once again, I felt mostly that Pappa was an underground detective, secretly uncovering dark mysteries in the night. These files were giving me that vibe. The files showed no signs of making my reading simpler. There were no names on any files. All of them were named, "Hope". *What? Again?!* I wondered how Pappa addressed them.

"Good morning Hope, how are you?" or "Hope you are doing well, hope" or "Hope, let us start with your session today. What have you got to offer?"

I was wondering too much, mocking Pappa's way of dealing with his patients. So, let us just come back to the files. Right, so no name on the files. The files obliged me by giving out the patient's house addresses. For a minute, I visually drew a hat on my head, a coat hanging on my shoulders, and spectacles on my eyes. Like a private eye collecting evidence, I drew a magnifying glass on my hand, as I read through all the addresses on the files. I should have had visually impaired myself at this point. The address on one of the files was ghastly. I could not comprehend it. But I would come back to that later. I did not want the burden of that one file to let down my morale of going through the remaining ones.

Thus, let us embark on the journey of these stories.

Part One

CHAPTER 3

A Forgetful Memory

Hi dear readers. I am "Hope". I lived a contended life but always wanted the best for my son. Hence, I went beyond my satisfied work life to always put in more efforts to make his life hopefully a little better than mine. We shared a great bond in our early ages. I did not want to be the Hitler father a son could have. With utmost affection and tender care, I brought up a son whom I would be proud of.

I had a small note always in my wallet. The note contained a small poem of how I envisioned me and my son's life.

The first part of the poem read on how our lives grow together from the lens of my eyes:

The journey unfolds,
that of me and my son.
The story here told,
the making of a son.

I stand, tall, dark, and handsome,
a few steps back, stands my son.
I toil for him, like a lion, fearsome.
Never enough that he says,
thanks a ton.

As years pass by my eyes,
I lead the way for him every day.
As years pass by his eyes,
he stands shoulder to shoulder,
My buddy.

The second part of the poem described the life that my son envisions in growing years of my age.

The journey commences,
that of me and my father.
The story here motivates,
the making of a leader.

I stand, tall, dark, and handsome,
a few steps back, stands my dad.
I toil for both our future, like a lion, fearsome.
Never enough that I say,
Thanks a ton.

As years pass by my eyes,
I followed the way he led me.
As years pass by his eyes,
he smiles to look at what he made of me.

Reality though was far from my shore of thoughts.

With old age, came more responsibilities and I became a burden to my son. Ours was a small family. Me, my son, my daughter-in-law, and my granddaughter. With the technological advancements, my next generation was becoming more culturally backwards. Respect was a far-lived island. Unknown would be a better fit. Life was fast-paced for the most part. The mornings were quick and the nights tiring. Within all the turbulence, there was one generation, luckily, who still had a similar lifestyle to mine. My granddaughter, whom I sweetly called Charu, named after my dead wife, was the only solace in my troubled old age. Charu was not like her parents. She spent time with me and loved to hear my yesteryear stories. Even though a few stories went on loop, she repeatedly asked for more. We went grocery shopping together and a few nights, she slept with me too while her parents were partying elsewhere. I used to drop her off at school every day. We liked that small walk we had together. She was good at her studies. I knew this because her marks were extraordinary even though her parents never sat with her to do homework. They probably never bothered to sit with her to understand her school life.

I knew her friends. Often at the school entrance, her friends would wait for us to just tell me, "Hi." Charu shared every detail of her school with me. I liked to hear them and sometimes, even warned her of any troublemakers. It would often follow with a word of advice or a potential life lesson.

She was a bright kid, particularly good at the implementation of my teachings.

This house was built with the cement of my sweat. Each drop's name was engraved on these walls. I was happy to live in the tiny room furnished for myself. My daughter-in-law cooked great food, and I never ever complained to her once. Despite minding my own business, my son felt like he had to tend to an extra person after my retirement. No income, more burden policy. My pension money was what I lived contented with. I never asked my son for any money. I did not know why I had become a load now. Nevertheless, I was treated like a nobody. They hardly spoke to me. And if they did, it was only about the property we peacefully lived in.

My routine did not disturb anyone. I took a walk in the park at 5 a.m.. Me and my friend briskly walked for a while and sat on a green-coloured bench daily. The topics of discussion were random. Mostly politics, sometimes sports, and seldom about our family matters. I would come back home, just in time to get ready to drop Charu at school, after which I would return to have breakfast. By then, my son and daughter-in-law would leave for their respective offices. After lunch, I picked up Charu again from school. The entire day after that lay in our hands for enjoyment. Stories would cook up. She danced sometimes. Independently, Charu would finish her homework too. Once my daughter-in-law was home, I would retire to my room and watch the TV. Post dinner, I sounded the sleeping bells.

File 1: Towards Hope

My son was unusually lovable the last night, happily chatting like we did during his teen years. I had such a great time with him that night. We cried over the death of his mother and sparkled over the birth of Charu. We laughed at his school days and hugged over his achievements. The talks were endless. Finally, before I was about to retire to my bed, my son asked me something.

"Dad, since we do not know how much time you would live, can you please sign this property paper so I can complete all the formalities soon?"

It was at that time I saw my daughter-in-law peeping from the door. She had heard all our conversations and was waiting for the right time. I then knew why all the chatting had come today. Nevertheless, the house was not meant for me. Nothing in this world is ours, except this body and our lovely soul. I came into this life with nothing. Shelter, food, and money were just means for me to keep that life alive. When I leave this life, off goes the body to mud and off goes all materialistic things to my future. And my future was my son and my granddaughter. Convinced of his manipulation, I agreed to sign the papers on an auspicious day, exactly on the day my son was born, a few days from now. They slept peacefully that night. I too probably slept, but I wished I had died in sleep.

The green bench waited for us, as usual. For some reason, today, I shared every bit of my family life with my friend. He heard me out patiently. When tears fell from my eyes, I could see the sadness on his face too. He promised to get me out of this unloving home.

"What about Charu?" I asked with concern. "I love her and so does she. Her heart will be broken. Moreover, who else will take care of her while her busy parents are out for work?"

The questions were endless in my mind. However, he promised to come up with a suitable solution soon. I trusted my questions more than my friend. The tape recorder of my mind kept reeling yesterday night's scenario with my son. It played forward and then backwards again. A few sentences played in slow motion while others zoomed fast. The tape-recorder played so many times that it came to a screeching halt at one point. My tape-recorder mind shut the cassette along with a broken heart.

I never went home that day. Only a few months later did my friend find me, in a state he could not imagine.

This is what my friend told me:

Charu's mom had dropped her at school that day, thinking you were probably doing extra rounds at the park. You never went back home from the park. Charu's mom had gotten a call from the school. You had not gone to pick her up from school either. Frustrated over your carelessness, Charu's mom left her work and stayed back at home with Charu. Your son was made aware of this in a while. As he had clients visiting his office, he told Charu not to worry.

"He might be in a friend's house. He will be back soon," cajoled your son to his wife.

"For so long?" enquired his wife, still angry to have left her office work unfinished.

"Let us wait for some time. He might have forgotten our phone numbers to inform," said your son.

"We need to get the property papers signed as early as possible before your dad forgets that he even built this house," the wife had decided with a stern face.

"Yeah, I gotta go now. My colleagues are waiting. We will discuss once I am home. Let us not wait till my birthday," signed off your son.

I got the call from your son, late at night. They had not heard anything from you. Worrying about the property slipping out of their hands more than you were missing, he enquired about your whereabouts to get your hands on the paper soon. I searched many places. Alas, I could not imagine a place you would go alone. I diligently expected you at the green bench daily, hoping one day you would pop up. Your son was hardly making any efforts, except calling me to ask for any updates on my search.

Alzheimer's had caught up to you. This condition is as good as death. It erases all the fruitful life memories. It prepares you for a fresh start, either in the same life or in the next. Initially, I was apprehensive to tell you about your family. So, I would visit you daily at the same green bench and slowly befriended you, again. You were happy with your son; you mentioned several times. He took good care of you. Things had changed for you and how! The old memories had dug a ditch. Fresh seeds were sowing in your life. I was gaining back my friend, like old times. The green bench had been painted freshly in the park. We went for the strolls and discussed anything but family. Even when I pursued small details about what you could tell me about your family, you only had praises. I was happy to have saved our friendship, until one day, suddenly you questioned, "How is Charu?" I lost you again.

CHAPTER 4

Lonely Traveller

My usual setting would be a morning cup of tea, sipping in the clear air, sitting on the small balcony attached to my room and scrutinising the on-lookers. Hoping someday, somebody would approach the gate and take me away, to what they called "Home". Ashraya was my home since I lost my parents. Their faces faded inside my memory files as I was too young. Since then, the old man had taken me into his shelter, like many other kids who yearned for loving parents rather than a home.

The old man had built the Ashraya foundation long ago, sheltering orphans. Some who were abandoned, and some, like me, who had lost their parents. Even though I called this home, it really was like a hostel. The old man did love all of us, and the food is great! But what I longed for, unlike others, are people whom I can address as mamma and pappa. And I will tell you why.

Schooling was never a problem for me. Being a bright student, a few scholarships here and there were helpful for me to sustain my study years. The problem were the students of the school. This goddam place's address, oh, how I loathed! In every application form, the address I would write started with "Ashraya Foundation". Instead of a parent's name, I would pen down the guardian's name. These screaming parents of students on the results day, oh, I hated them too! The old man managed to attend the parent-teacher meeting. He was good at nodding his head and assuring me that I had no complaints from the teachers. I followed the first-in, first-out principle for such meetings. I did not have the courage to meet anybody else's eyes. Not that the students teased me. They were more than sympathetic. Pitying myself was okay for me but when others did, it added to the burning fire. The sight of children happily conversing with their parents made my heart crumble a little, day by day. There was a vacuum in my heart that nobody noticed to fill up. There was nobody I could go crying to. The old man told me a few convincing words daily but that is about the time he would give anyone. He had to cater to a hundred other crying kids.

I would silently wet the bed (not by pissing on it) and let the good dreams seep in to control the outburst of my tears. And the next day would still be the same. On the weekends, the balcony looked over a young lad, full of dreams, hoping he would find a home. There would hardly be any visitors. But on the days they arrived, I would dress myself, fit enough for a professional job, keeping a confined smile on my face, and eyes glittering and wanting to be taken. Then, that night, I would wet the bed again.

Years passed by, and the balcony got familiar with the scent of my emotions. Over the years, I had seen many of them opt for adoption. Not me. I was not even an option now. The old man said that I had a temper that no parent would welcome.

I tried to win over the arguments we frequently had by saying, "I am going to tell them that the temper is built up from the lack of love. Will their love not free my heart of this anger?"

The old man did not retort but neither did he inform me of any visitors. The dormitory bore a deserted look. Many left with parents, many left to follow their dreams, and many left for their jobs in other cities. And here I was, reigning like a king in this uninhabited palace, still searching for parental love. I monkeyed around the house often, unable to concentrate on anything else.

The old man was not entertaining new orphans either because he was ageing and could not tend to small children like he used to. I was too high-priced for maintenance. With a comfortable job at hand, I did give him a part of my salary so he could feed us sufficiently. But that was about all the interaction we had. My anger turned to blame over a period. This old man did nothing to get me adopted! He showed all the other children to parents. He hardly introduced me to prospective parents. Why? Why did he do this to me alone? If you put the logic in place, I was the one who craved the most. I really wanted a name for my parents. He should have let me go first. Why did he hold me back? We often fought over this. His age no longer allowed my anger to flow in. He often ignored me. But he would always end with one serene sentence.

"*Beta*, you can stay here for as long as you like. This is your home."

"That is a lame excuse to keep me here, *baba*," I retorted.

File 2: Towards Hope

The old man handed me a visiting card. Oh wow, maybe, somebody had noticed my balcony finally! My happiness knew no bounds. I was in a trance. I wondered what they look like. I will have a nice name for my house address now. I will never write a guardian's name. Ah! I was an orphan no more. Only when the old man shook my shoulder did I come back from the far away land I had already gone into. With one look, he pointed his index finger at the visiting card and left. Yes, I forgot to see the name on the card. It had a name and a profession—therapist. It felt good that I was being adopted by a doctor (at least I felt so). I ran back to the old man.

"So, when do I shift?" I had enquired. "Will you be coming to get me, or should I go myself?"

I was a twenty eight year old grown-up man, but as excited as a child. I was already planning to wear a blue shirt and a black pant. It suited me well. I was going to shave my beard this morning anyway. The old man sensed again that I had flowed into fantasy land.

Stone-faced, he informed me, "Beta, he is not going to adopt you. He is going to treat you. Look, I am also getting older. You need someone to guide you. Maybe he can."

That is when I met the therapist.

The sessions were going well. Not that there was any improvement from my side. But the therapist made sure I was listening to him. He advised a few tactics to control my anger. Not that I did. But the time I spent with him; I was happy. Once he showed me a different light.

"Dear Hope, while you are grieving of being parentless, have you seen parents being childless?" That did not make sense.

"How can parents be childless? They are parents because they have children, right? What makes you say that?" I had asked like a child again.

He chuckled. "Son, they are childless because they have been kicked out of their own home, by their own children. After all the love they showered and gave them a good education, the old people are driven away from the only life they toiled for day and night. Old people are seen as a burden now, my child."

I left that session with a lot of thoughts in my mind. I could not fathom the cruelty on these parents.

My guardian, the old man, died of a heart attack. I lit the fire on his pyre, and for once, I felt like his child. We were there for each other, always. Maybe I was his favorite child and that was the reason why he never let me go? Yes, I did take care of him and he did take care of me too. We were like the father and son duo, who loved each other so much and yet did not confide much. Silently, maybe that is what we were—a father and a son. Because his will had only one name: mine. Ashraya was to be handed over to me. It had always been my home and will be. Stupid of me to think otherwise.

I was drenched in rain when he had picked me up from the streets. Here I stand in front of the house again, drenched, not in rain but in the clouds of guilt. The old man and I, we were the only two left in this house for a few years. And it had never struck me that we could have made a great pair as a father and son. Should I have taken care of his health? I was so engrossed in my own pain that I had never held his hand to know how he was. I had been inhuman to my guardian parent. The doctor was right. Parents can be childless too. Someone who is a replica of me. I had not cared enough for the old man while he had given up on his own life to tend to our growing years. The guilt blinded me to all the earthly pleasures I once wanted in life. At this point in life, I did not know the purpose of my stay here. I had always had a guardian's name. And now I didn't even have that. Ashraya was my only "forever together" now. I had overlooked the beauty of this home for long. Today, my eyes were clear. Or were they?

I shot my eyes towards the dark grey sky and whistled a sorry to the old man. As I lowered my eyes in slow motion,

I scanned my home, the Ashraya Foundation, from top to bottom. In the twilight hours, it looked no less than a mansion. It bewildered me that I had not once gone up to the terrace. You would ask why I was here today. My dear reader, you should have guessed it by now. Without the old man, whom I thought of now as more of a father, I did not know what to do in life. I was like that lost drenched child again. I might as well go along with the old man. Maybe, if there is anything called rebirth, I will have parents. So, here I am, standing at the edge of the terrace, also viewing the setting sun diminishing all hopes of life as darkness hugs me. Here is where my clear eyes failed to see the small glimmer of light even in the darkness that fell on the whole city like a blanket, offering cosy and dreamy nights. Light and darkness are synonymous with our life. Each one promising the onset of the other. But me? My eyes were clear, right? I readied myself for my destination. A small stone dropped lifeless as it hit the ground from the terrace. Wasn't it already like that and thus called a stone? That was my life anyway, feeling like a stone. Let us end it too. I flew one leg off the terrace, occupying the space between my life and death.

CHAPTER 5

Can You Hear Me?

"Happy birthday to you, happy birthday day to…happy birthday to you."

And a roaring applause would follow.

"She has such a sweet voice," every teacher commended.

This was the usual routine every day in the school assembly. You know, there are these extra groups in school for anything *not* study-related? I had applied for the news-reading. But here I was, in full force, singing happy birthday to you. Because my voice is sweet? Please, just let me read the news. But no. Not that I did not like singing, but that mic was something else for me.

Hi, I am Hope. At a young age, I harboured an interest in journalism. I loved dancing with words. I watched the news on a regular basis and was awed by their endless and lightning-speed flow of words. Not to forget the presence of mind, fact-finding, and having mindful debates. Since the knowledge of journalism itself is limited at a schooling age, I really did not know what journalism meant, except that if I did become one, I might one day be the bearer of all the news around the world or be that one editor whose story writing would inspire people from all walks of life. I wanted to interview people; poor ones, and rich ones, and give a grand entry of their lives into others by letting their story known. Media can thus be powerful in this way too.

Dictionaries were my friend. Often, I would use complicated words with my parents. The joy of explaining to them the meaning was a treat to me. The glossary of my words grew with each sunrise that I witnessed. Even a small eventful day at home would get written in my diary. I read a lot of books, mostly thrillers. What makes a good story is not to just narrate it but how it is told. Even a simple story, if twisted, can make a great suspense story. An echo of claps would be heard at home when I orated a small piece of my writing to my parents.

Only in the later stages of schooling did I realise that journalism had many facets to it, one being—studying the subjects of economics, civics, history, etc. These subjects were like the sandpit; the more I tried to help myself out, the more it tried to pull me in. There was no escape from my dislike of these subjects. Hence, I had to shelve my dreams of journalism. Journalism also required speaking and thankfully, writing did not. My voice was not lauded anyway. It missed the rhythm. Modulations were far from happening. My emotions were not in the right place. And I knew, my physical voice had transformed to another way of voicing, writing.

It was during 11th grade that I penned my first poem. The train went on from there, non-stop. My mother helped me enter a few contests that would publish my poems in international editions of anthologies. My English teacher was perplexed at my writings and the management of those to find myself in books. She, like any other teacher, would urge the need for the poems to be read and recognised in larger forums. Unfortunately, my voice was becoming a hindrance, again. I had to recite my own poem because obviously, it is my poem, my emotions. At a class hearing, my own classmates could not grasp the right amount of sharpness and loudness in my voice. The poem engrossed a lot of emotions, as it was written on the taboo of being born a girl in our Indian society. But my voice did not ooze the same. Finally, a boy from my class had to read *my* poem. Obviously, the emotions did not strike the right chord. Only the sharpness and loudness of his voice were measured right.

My diary filled up, page to page. I did not make it see the light of the day. Neither did I produce the right sentiment, nor did I want anyone else to patronise it. Only I, and I alone patrolled my poems. I had reached the 100th mark no sooner than the completion of my 12th grade. Even in college, I tried to pursue and put forth my poems wherever possible. The devil lies within me, and right where the voice matters.

No soothing words from my mother helped to curb the fire in me. Slowly and maturely, my genre of poems adjusted to the situations of my own life. While I wrote about butterflies, freedom fighters, and friendships during school and college, I now write about stronger, deeper, and conscious feelings. Professionally, I was doing so well but buried inside me was always the writer. For reasons known, life moved on, getting promoted both professionally and personally.

I believe that there are times in our lives when our inner passions get triggered due to externally applied upsetting behaviour. It came in my life too. That is when the pen huddled the diary again. I wrote and wrote until the tears from my eyes vanished into the words of my poems. But again, these poems were hidden within the walls of my safe.

In life, I struggled to let my voice be exposed. What I hid from people was how strong the voice was pitched in my writings.

File 3: Towards Hope

My mother was the only one who understood my talent. Even though she did not know about my diary, she knew something was biting me from inside. To get all the built-up anger out, she introduced me to this therapist.

He was a nice person. Perhaps I liked him because not only did he extol my "sweet" voice, but he gave it a hearing. Many days, he made me read my poems. A poem I wrote when I was happy, a poem in sadness, a poem of friendships, and likewise many others, each session. When I read, he would close his eyes and allow all the emotions to flow into him. Once I was done, he would heave a low sigh and always said only one word, "Wow". It baffled me as to how he got the sentiment bang on! Never had I seen anyone being so engrossed in my poems and enjoying them with each word.

He trained me to think differently: "Am I reading to the right audience in the first place? Not everyone understands the nitty-gritty of poems. Only a true artist will hail the praises of another one. Others just criticise to hide their inability to perceive the talent."

This did make sense.

"The emotions of the book lie with the reader, dear Hope. Similarly, what you orate is up to the listener to consume. It is not your fault," he had told me matter-of-factly. "And if the reader or listener cannot blow the right amount of emotion into it, they will never appreciate art. Hence, it is equally important to find the right audience for your talent."

I was going to the therapist for a problem that had grown like a mole with me from a young age. His sessions were helping me to voice my opinions even more. Open mics were a good place to start as an introduction. Eventually, I became a regular. It was an unbiased audience. My poems had met their soulmates. The echoes of the clapping filled a larger room now. My voice had found a kingdom and my writing, its disciple.

I wondered sometimes if I should talk about my marriage with the therapist. It was hitting a rough patch. The ingredients of most of my writings stemmed from being in an incompatible relationship. The anger, the hurt, and the irritation, all washed away in the depths of my writings. I was not able to give my opinion, was bossed over and subdued. These, again, tied to my childhood of not being heard when my voice lay unworthy.

The feeling of being unheard came back like it was just yesterday. A train drove past me. It showed me singing Happy Birthday. Then, the mocking. Then, I wrote. I wrote again. The pages of my diary flipped. My mom was clapping. I had ditched studying journalism. I wrote. I struggled to write a few pieces as my pen dried up. I frantically searched for a pen. My diary clouded up. I could not reach it. Words were falling. The alphabets were haywire. I screamed for help. I jolted forward out of my bed, sweating, and dreaded of the thought of losing my diary and pen. I was as good as dead without them. The nightmares became a regular. The relationship was soaring. I skipped my sessions with the doctor on the pretext of open mics. Well, I skipped those too. My diary lay in one corner, untouched for a month. I was not respected. Neither did I respect myself.

That one day, when my heart oozed my mindless thinking, it created a vacuum of space that showed me where I could be happier. I will leave this world in its entirety and travel to a place unknown, but happy. Finally, I would alleviate my soul of all the dreams I stitched. But there was one last thing to do. Words were failing me. Somehow, I managed to put it together. My last poem, called, "The Unheard". And this, I would expose to everyone. Being a writer, I needed some drama, even in the face of death.

I placed the knife, my last poem, and myself on the couch for one last sitting together. I decided to slit my throat as that is what has given me hurt more than anything else, my voice. I swayed the knife from left to right near my neck, measuring the intensity and quickness needed. While playing with the knife, I got a small cut on my hand and blood spilled out. A dew of blood dropped on the title of my last poem and hid the two main letters of it, "Un". Now, the title read to the naked eye as, "The heard". One will have to look closely to spot the stained "Un". Nevertheless, it will dry up soon, just as will I.

CHAPTER 6

An Injury to Inspire

3… 2… 1… the bullet shot is heard. Nervousness had spun over to determination and off I swam to the final lap. I could see the touch point along with my opponent who was almost ready to touch it. I did an extra powerful push. The TV repeatedly played the final touchdown, each time in different angle. My opponent had celebrated a bit too early, slowing down before the winning touch. I had zoomed past him and won it by a fraction of a millisecond.

Hi, I am Hope, and rightly so. I am a swimmer. I won the selection round to the national competition. I inched more towards my big dreams. I was now housed in the sports complex, ready to get the training started for nationals!

In my younger days, I was trained in a small village. The village's lake was the arena. Growing up, I was always eager to know about the techniques to win competitions. We were a joint family but during the Olympics season, nobody dared to touch the TV remote. I was always inspired by the many sports on display. The winning country's national anthem playing at the end gave me goosebumps every time. I wanted to be there, head held high, singing our national anthem.

My teacher from school pestered me to try for the selection round to nationals. Till the state level, it was a breeze for me. To train for the national levels, I had to shift to the sports complex, designated to pop out star players. The building was a mini city in itself. Acres and acres of land swarmed with sportsmen and sportswomen. For a few days, I would just wander around, exploring the details of this city. The apartments were well-furbished and enough for a good night's sleep. For the days held the training in different complexes for different sports. Few of the sports were combined under one structure. There is hardly any chance that you can spot a person one day and see him again the next day. Unless, of course, if you are training in the same building.

Apart from rigorous swimming sessions, I had to contend with my own body to keep it fit. Physical fitness, while I was geared up for, mental soundness was equally trained for. Yoga was introduced to bring calmness, breathing strategies, and control our negative expressions while running through a race. My diet plan was stricter. All planned. Every week, a therapy session attendance was a must. I went through a series of tests, each time a different theme to it. Failure to succeed in any of these tasks brought upon the dark cast of being dropped out of the nationals.

I would not say the training was tough, but I knew my strength, and that was physical. My weakness lay in my mental stability. So, I had to put in extra time and effort in yoga and therapy sessions. A few more months, and I would be *the* package needed for nationals.

Like me, there were selected contestants in the complex, getting trained accordingly in other areas of sports. I usually kept to myself and did not make any friends. There were a few others who chilled out after their training and hung with each other to brush off any stress. I had dipped into the swimming area late night, trying to get my breathing at the right pace. Unaware of my presence, I heard the boys gossiping about me!

One of them initialised the conversation, saying, "Hey, you know that swimmer? I have hardly seen him with anybody else. Keeps to himself."

Another one agreed. "Yes. I would not be like that if I wanted to relieve some stress from those training sessions. It is rigorous man. I need friends like you, just to chalk out the entire day."

Another one, being investigative, "I wouldn't compare us with him. It could be a possibility that the guy needs more training. He might be a master in the main trade, but without support staff, the trade doesn't bloom well." Everyone had nodded their heads simultaneously, agreeing to his stupid conclusion.

One sensible guy muttered, "Guys, don't judge him. We don't even know that guy!" Unable to concentrate on my breathing, I purposefully splashed out of the water, leaving a trail of my ego in the water for them to look.

I walked up to my towel, straight face, as though I did not hear anything. One of the guys, immediately regretted, "Oops. He was here!"

The spy did not shy away. "Hey, swimmer! Were you tasting the water all this while? I wonder if you ever studied that water is tasteless, just like you."

Few of them tried to shush him but other few laughed hard with him.

"I was practising my breathing exercise," I replied calmly, putting my yoga training into use.

The spy hit back, prompting, "Ah! Why don't you talk at all? Come on man, we are your friends." And another burst of provocation hit my face.

I tried hard, "Leave me alone. I like it that way."

One guy walked straight towards me, meeting me by the eye. His nose had almost touched mine. My eyes clearly showed my nervousness.

"We too like you," he whispered. "That is why we won't leave you alone." He stepped back and walked towards his set of friends, not looking back even once.

It was an eerie feeling. I might have wetted my bottoms. But who cares, I was anyway wet from the swim. My self-confidence was the one actually drenched. I had to walk past them to go to my room. I could not gather any courage. Head bent down, I tried to scoot as fast as I could. Alas, it was one against a gang. They pushed me while I was trying to create a maze between them so I could run away. They hit my shoulders hard. One tried lifting my leg. One tried to pull my hand towards him. One tickled me on the hips. Ultimately, I landed right into my peace-giver: water. Again. Fresh bubbles of laughter could be heard.

File 4: Towards Hope

The mocking continued daily. All my training was failing, except, of course, my strength—swimming. It was like my birthmark, not escaping me, staying, and growing strong inside of me. All else that was strung to me, because the "training" required to be "passed" in all aspects of a sportsman, vanished slowly from me.

My swim trainer was happy. My dietician was happy. They knew I was ready for the finals. At the far end of the room, there were guys that gave me looks of jealousy. They were not happy as I inched closer towards my goal every day.

At this point, I really needed to talk to my coach about my mental well-being.

I had told him, "I am being bullied. It is not in my character to speak back or get into fights. But that does not mean I am not hurting from inside. Coach, I need help here. They are getting into my head."

My coach was surprised, and asked, "Aren't you attending sessions with our in-house consultant?"

"I am making the psychiatric session difficult, for both of us," I answered honestly. "I do not give a good ear to him, but give a mouthful of hurt from my side. Nothing that he is telling me is deepening in my mind. There are people clobbering my mind. Water is my only survival partner. Why didn't the therapist understand this? Their primary job is to understand people, right? Read their mind, write down our emotions, be our listening outpost and things like that. Why is he suggesting things that I do not care about? Why is he also pushing me to talk to them? Why isn't he concentrating on my strength? Does this same guy coach those mockers too? Why isn't he telling them anything? You got my frustration, right? Too many questions, very few or rather no answers."

My coach gave it a good one minute thought as I stood there, awaiting a solution. Even as I stood waiting, I tried persuading him.

"Coach, I came here to learn. My family has high hopes. These competitions and winning them will make our life better. I want to…"

And he had cut me off, "Shhh, I have a solution. Wait. Patience, my boy. I was thinking it out. I need to think fairly for all my players and yet help all of them."

I persisted impatiently, "What do I do then?"

The coach had finally said, "I will talk to my therapist friend and see if he can help you out. He is not trained to be a sports consultant but as a general advisor, he might be able to help you."

I just shook my coach's hand and left the scene, feeling a sense of relief.

When I first met the therapist, he did not talk about my coaching, swimming, or the bullying, which I had made very clear. But, maybe that is what made me comfortable with the therapist. He held a personal Midas touch.

"Why do you think people are bullying you?" he finally asked me one day.

I was not ready with an answer. I was never ready with one. I just felt bullied.

"I don't know. They just keep teasing me," I replied.

"Do you feel it is because of your background or because they see you as a strong competitor?" he probed.

For the first time, I did not have answers. But I had to respond.

"Sir, I never gave it this thought. Our coaches are the same, so in all fairness, all of us are equally competent. And background too, they never talked about it. I do not socialise much. That's it."

He provided an explanation, saying, "Maybe they want you to talk to them. Often, people do not realise they are bullying. It might be normal for them. It might be their mechanism to come closer to you. Have you ever voiced to them that you feel bullied? Other than telling me and your coach?"

I sat, unmoving.

"I will leave you to that thought today," he said, patted on my back and left the session.

For a few days, those mockers were out of sight. That was strange. Maybe my therapist had requested them to stay away from me. But obviously it meant good for me. Out-of-sight, out-of-mind. Strange workings of the mind. It then troubled me even more. Curiosity got the hang of me. Why weren't the guys meeting? Probably their matches were scheduled. They probably needed more practice on their game rather than gossiping about a nobody like me. He is probably counselling the other boys now.

After one such gruelling session on what makes a "sportsman", by the understanding therapist, I went for a swim. Only water calmed me down like itself. Because the mind was a conglomeration of angry waves, hitting each other and finally dropping to the same troubled point, not moving on to other silent shores. I was in chaos. The very thought of not seeing the troublesome guys anymore was pricking me more than my mind could take. My mind was churning with assumptions. Probably they had already won their match. Maybe they were planning something big for me. Better would be if they were expelled due to their unruly behaviour. Hopefully, the guys themselves had finally realised their mocking. It was going overboard. The therapist put some good into these bad people. But all my assumptions started with "hope", "maybe", "probably", and "mostly", not sure of what could have transformed them.

I sank in my own feelings, unable to let others know about them. I could not train my mind yet. That is the primary reason they could play with my mind. Concentration and focus are the core of sports, which, unfortunately, I was losing to. While I was still contemplating my assumptions, I thought one of the guys zoomed past me. I did a quick turn to my back. Nope, nobody was there. I was hallucinating, was my first thought. I turned back to my front, ready to leave it all behind and start my swim. Strikingly, towering over the swimming pool was him. He stared blankly, directly into my eyes, again. Fearing what was worst to come, I ducked inside the pool. I would stay inside as long as I could.

The water was good. I held my breath. I could hear the guys outside. I stayed put inside the water. I just sat at the centre, holding my breath. This time, I was sure and prayed to God to take my breath away, to keep me in a happy place. I did not struggle for a pinch of breath too. I let the bubbles float away from my body.

CHAPTER 7

Digital Love

At the age of twenty eight, unmarried, I was dead against arranged marriages. I did not understand the whole concept of it. My parents were searching profusely.

"The younger, the better," they said. "You will get a young girl while you are young too."

Apparently, I was already old for marriage according to my parents. My mom always carried a photo of mine. She loved attending functions because that is where the prospects are higher. She showed it to people like it was her Aadhar card. And if I had gone to the function too, I was the live Aadhar card! She used to just push me right in front of the aunties.

"Mom, they are not blind yet, they can scan me from afar," I used to rebuke her. She shushed me every time and her hand would so stiffly be wraped around mine that someone could play tug-of-war from the other hand. Often, she would provide vague introductions.

"Beta, you remember Shika aunty na? You always used to play around her saree's pallu. She has a lovely daughter. You would pull her hair and run away. Remember? Remember?"

"I don't care, Mom!" I would whisper in her ears and vanish. As much as I hated attending ceremonies, the food stall was where I would vanish to. I made great efforts to feed my stomach, slowly. I relished each bite of all delicacies while my mother was busy acquainting herself with guests. If they had a daughter of a young age, they soon became her friends and their phone number would get added to her phone. If not, tata and bye-bye.

A monthly visit to our family astrologer was a must. I sat disinterested.

My mom and dad would fold their hands and blurt out the clichéd dialogue, "Please find a suitable girl for our son."

"How does this guy know that this particular girl only is suitable for me?" I had argued.

She scolded me for being disrespectful towards a system of knowledge, "Beta, only if the stars match is it considered good. You both will live happily ever after. And the more the numbers match, the happier you will be."

"Mamma, happily ever after happens only in books and movies," I had continued arguing. "In real life, it is up to a husband and a wife to make a marriage work."

Her ears then concentrated on the astrologer. He never ran out of photos. He shovelled them like a game of cards. So much for gambling with *my* life.

One day, Mom came to me with enthusiastic vibes.

"Beta, Pooja Aunty was telling me that now, there are online matrimony sites? Is it true?" she asked. "Can we search a girl through online platforms?"

I cursed that aunty and replied, "Yes, mamma. But they are not good."

Mothers are not the giving-up type, you see. "Arrey no. Pooja told me they are incredibly good. Girl's photos are also uploaded it seems along with required details like Gothra, occupation, height, etc. And lot of options she said. *Chalo*, let us register in all the sites she has given me."

I tried to sneak away on the pretext of work. Who said it was easy? Pooja Aunty had given a list of five sites for registration. We started with the first one. I opened the site. Mom said she would dictate what to write, and I would just go on typing it. That is a wonderful idea! I need not take those troubles. She started reading out my height, age, gothra, and parent's occupation, and I blindly typed. When she had read out my occupation, I jumped up on the bed.

"Mamma, what is this? I am an Engineer. I do not know the C of CA.."

Guiltily, she replied, "Oh sorry, beta. Whatever Pooja Aunty has given, I am telling you the same thing. Let us continue."

"Mamma, this is cheating," I tried explaining to her. "What else has she fed inside your brain?"

I snatched the sheet of paper from her. In the hobbies section were listed: travelling, painting, and dancing.

I pin-pointed this. "What is this? None of these are my hobbies. You know that I only love to hang out with my friends or sleep. These are my only two hobbies."

She signaled to go further. "It is okay. Girls like such things it seems. And how can friends and sleep be a hobby? They are just necessities of life. Let us move on."

With lot of disagreements, she won over all my cases and finally we had registered on one site. Seemed like she had a lot of time that day.

"Aren't you going to cook lunch today?" I had quipped,

She smiled. "After we are done with this. This is the next site," she said and pointed her finger on the sheet.

"Mamma, I will fill all of them today. It is the same information na. You carry on with your work."

Convinced, she left, "Ok! Alright! But finish it today so we can start getting calls from tomorrow. We can also start the search. It is an auspicious day. And do not forget to upload a good photo. You look good in formals. Upload any one of such photos. Girls are going to fall flat."

Excitedly, she left the room, the sheet of paper, and me with my laptop. Thanks to Photoshop and other similar apps, I bloated my photo from top to bottom. I looked like a fat uncle rather than a thin, young boy. I uploaded this made-up photo of mine on all sites and vowed never to come back to these sites. Mom wondered why proposals were not coming from the online matrimony sites.

I smiled cunningly. "I told you! These are not good. Pooja Aunty is lying."

The target, Pooja Aunty, was banished from my mother's network of marriage-related soldiers.

Nevertheless, the ones that still came through different means, I would reject proposals deliberately. Even examinations take three hours to think and write. And even after that, there is no guarantee that you will pass. Then, how can you pass a girl within a few minutes of meeting her? For obvious reasons, she will put her best foot forward for those few minutes. What about when she gets angry? What is her take on intimacy? What bothers her in life? Does she have career aspirations too? I am sure that one person cannot bring all the answers to all my questions in a few ticks of the clock. And these are just a few questions. Being the traditional mom, nothing else was more concerning than feeding a young, unmarried child.

Mom had her ways of hunting and so did I. You name any matrimony site, a broker, or a book in a temple, I was everywhere! Proposals stormed. To avoid the ones mom sent, I would ask uncomfortable questions to these young girls, when the time was right.

And that time is: "Do you two want to talk in private and get to know each other?"

That was when I bombarded them with uncomfortable questions. They would happily reject me. Mom was perturbed. How can someone reject such a nice man? I was not handsome but suitably worthy from all quarters. Little did she know her son had a back door. I was registered to this site called, "Finding Forever". This was just the site I needed. It was kind of like blind dating. Because the site did not accept any photos, neither on the profile nor sending it to anyone by chat. You could enter all your details in the personal information of the site but only your nickname would be visible to others. Not until you and the girl, both click on the "Meet" button, would the actual details about each other be revealed. Here too, no photos were shown though. Your actual name, phone number, and address are unmasked. Once the identities were out to the other party, the profiles get deleted from the site automatically within a few hours.

The site really allowed me to know a person rather than loving their beauty. I applied a lot of filters on my profile and hence, very few girls would qualify that meet the criteria. I chatted with quite a few daily. The moment any girl asked for my photo too soon or clicked on the "Meet" button, I blocked them. If I were to be a one-woman man, I would need time for a person and fall in love with who the person is.

Sakshi was that one. We did not have a lot in common, but we respected each other's opinions. We used to fight online and get back together. We shared our deepest secrets. We knew what life we wanted. Everything was sorted. The only thing left was the proposal. It was late at night. Today, I wanted to propose. She came online right when she was on my mind too. Now in my heart too. I had my message ready, even before chatting about anything else. I had seen her "typing..." for an exceedingly long time and wondered what she had to tell me. I could not control my excitement.

It will either be a yes or a no. Anyway, we did not know our faces, our names, and anything at all except our personalities. A no could mean nothing at all. What is the possibility of finding her in real life? I did the math mentally. She was still "typing…" I pressed enter on my keyboard at the same time she did. The screen shone brightly on our messages, and both read, "Will you marry me?" This was a love story, fortunately, neither me nor Sakshi needed answers. It was unmistakable. The thoughts were aligning similarly. With one more press of a button, both of us hit the "Meet" button at the same time.

File 5: Towards Hope

Sakshi came to my home first with her parents. We had not met each other after the proposal as she wanted to now go through the formal and traditional route of seeing each other. My mom was overjoyed. I hid behind the door like a girl would do. Sakshi had long, wavy hair. Her eyes like sparkling water. Her smile, breath-taking. If beauty had a definition, it was coined after her. In my mind, I had already written a poem. She looked all over my house. Probably searching for me. I wished mom called me early. It felt like a lifetime now! Finally, my mom called for me. While Sakshi's eyes wandered to which door I would pop out of, I walked towards her, manly enough that I could be. Shoulders straight, head held high. That shyness of her smile lit a fire inside me. The elders were discussing something more about marriage. I was fixated on her. Her eyes still wandered around my home though, strangely.

After a few hours, the girl's party left. I walked back to my room, balloons bursting, bubbles popping, and instruments playing. I waited for her call. And dozed off too soon, dreaming about Sakshi. After the dream ended, which was not too long, I woke up smiling, still thinking of Sakshi. I checked my phone but there were no messages from Sakshi. I called her and while I was waiting for her to pick up the call, my mom entered my room. Her face told me she was not having a good day today. She informed me that Sakshi's parents had called to tell her that they could not move ahead with the alliance as the horoscopes did not match. My mom had shown the horoscope too and there was nothing wrong she was told by our priest. This was an unexpectedly strange rejection. My mind went blank. Did her parents not like me? I was ready to talk more.

I gave a ring to Sakshi again. She cut the call. I opened WhatsApp to message her and saw her "typing…" This time I waited for her words.

She had pinged me the following, "I saw a photo in your home. It disturbed me. When I asked your mom whose photo it was, she said it was your great-grandfather's photo. It was disheartening for me to know. Hope you had told me about it sooner. It is devastating for me."

Now, it all made sense for the rejection. I started to type something in my justification. I erased it and did not respond to her. What is the use of making a person understand something for which they have already derived a conclusion? I threw the phone away after deleting her number. I went out to the living room and stared at my great-grandfather's photo. He had had a skin discolouration problem, called vitiligo. It may have been hereditary, but nothing had passed on for three generations! Goddammit, Sakshi! Neither my grandfather nor my father suffered from anything like that. You saw me, there were no skin problem on me. Oh, you were worried that what if our child gets one? Wow. I thought I knew you. Of all the things that you could look for in a family, we scored well but all you choose to see is the photo of my dead great-grandfather and his skin condition. Her constant prying around the house made sense now.

Nothing mattered to me now. This was not even a dream I could incur. Soon, I looked like a Devadas, which I was by the way. My mom could not bear my sight. She continued her ways of searching and this time, I did not stop her.

We had headed out to my cousin's marriage. We were likely to stay there for a few days. It was an open-air wedding. The mandap was set up right in the middle of a sprawling grassland that overlooked a sea. The hotel stood behind. A beautiful sight but nobody to cherish it with. The festivities began without much ado. My mom had forced me to get busy with something and more importantly to be cheerful. That could not be forced though. Anyway, I went ahead with getting myself busy by doing some wedding preparations. The next day was the wedding. Everything was set. Early morning, the bride and the groom will be two bodies and one soul.

I crept up to the mandap late into the sleepy night. The pyre sat there, waiting for its burn the next day. No, it cannot wait until the next day. It was going to burn for all good things the next day. But this was the time to gobble all the negativity to ashes. I had lit the pyre. I was going to be yours. Burn me like you have not burnt for a long time. The fire in me was lit again for other reasons. Only you can appease the pain to ashes. Let it be done now. The right leg is auspicious. I raised my left leg to be consumed by this fire. Someone pulled me back. Oops, left leg, ill fate. I should have put my right leg forward to end this auspiciously.

I turned back in anger with the same fire in my eyes. "Who the hell are you? Why did you stop me?"

An old man stood calmly, smiling, as though I had seen God. Oh, maybe I am already dead.

"What were you doing?" he inquired.

I realised something then. "You saved me."

Though he was surprised, he replied calmly, "Oh! This was suicide? I am sorry to have disturbed you in the process. Now that I have saved you, care to tell me your story?"

I said "yes," meekly. I liked visiting the therapist then after. Here was one person who had cared to listen to my entire love story and feel for me.

Continuing Towards Hope

The therapist probed my inner consciousness to evacuate all the hate and to forget the entire love ordeal. He knew any more small triggers would take me back to the realm of suicidal tendencies. Hence, he spaced his suggestions at the right time for healing.

First, he did tell me to spend time alone, and re-think the entire situation, without anger or betrayal in mind. I had started hating the whole concept of love. I had never responded to Sakshi's bizarre claims and hence, there was no closure from my end. The angst had carried forward and built up inside me.

Secondly, he persuaded me to talk to my parents. I had confessed to mom about me seeing a therapist.

"You mean, you are in love with a therapist?" She had enquired worriedly.

"Arrey, no ma. I am seeing a therapist, it does not mean dating. And it is a he. I go to him for sessions. For an unbiased hearing. Time will heal me. Trust it," I comforted her.

Mom was very understanding. For the time being, the girl hunting was on hold. She knew I would take time to get back to normalcy.

Third, the therapist advised me to spend time with my friends and follow anything that I was passionate about. My friends were sympathetic, yes but over time, we just laughed it off. It was a foolish decision anyway. Who blind dates a girl, gives direct entry to home, and then expects everything to be perfect for a marriage? Love does not marry easily. If it does, it will come along with many hardships.

I did not have any hidden talents, per se. But what is the harm in learning a new art form? I did all of it, and to my own surprise, I was able to get out of my own depressed grave.

I had survived a love failure. I had survived an almost suicide mission. I lived to tell this tale.

* * *

The house was buzzing with people. Our relatives had come home to attend my cousin's marriage. In one of the rooms, all the aunties had gathered to chit-chat. In another room, the men were gathered with their beer bottles. My cousins and I had went out for a late-night movie, without the bride, of course. She was too busy chatting away with her would-be-hubby.

The wedding did not invite any unpleasant activities, as yet. With everyone happy about the new alliances, they retired to their respective rooms. Next day, post a small function and a reception at night, everyone would retire to their normal routine. Little did anyone forethought of what could happen to me. I was feeling uneasy throughout the wedding ceremonies. Maybe it was just the whole atmosphere of marriages. Something shrunk inside me every time I saw the auspicious fire. Ah, that was my heart. It ached. That pyre should have been mine long ago, in my marriage. And now it is going to write somebody else's name on it. In the dead of the night, unknown to me, I walked up to the mandap. Last time, it was a conscious decision to burn myself in it. This time though, I cannot imagine why my sub-conscious failed to drive me away from this curse of death. This time, I lit the fire, and luckily put my right foot forward. So, here it is. Finally, the end of it. I hoped I would find true love in my next birth if there is any.

The raging fire was welcoming. I think I saw God now, for real. She was running towards me. With a paper in her hand. What is that? Maybe an entry pass to heaven. She held my hand. Now, she would take me to the heavens and in our next birth, hopefully, we reunite. I followed her religiously to the gates of heaven. The pyre had doused my search for love and with it, took the ashes of my pain.

CHAPTER 8

The Hanging Payals

Hi, I am Hope. Dear reader, I hoped you would come back to read my story after an hour or so because that is exactly the time, I must finish my practice. Once dad came back from office, that same room housed an uncomfortable silence. Although mom was supportive, she did not have the courage to face dad's decisions. With his rage came words that were only meant to be unheard. He loved me like any father would. It was not love or remotely any respect from my side though.

We come from a conservative family. The only extracurricular activities that girls like me are allowed are singing, dancing, or painting. Our world seem to be limited to a few art forms and that too only to be pursued as hobbies. As the elders call it, "something to keep us occupied for few hours". I was put through the same ordeal. My real talent though stemmed from my dance classes. I practised

Bharatanatyam and contemporary fusion dance. I was always eager to attend the dance class. I was an average student at school and compensated for that loss in my dance. For all dance performances in schools or inter-school competitions, I would not only participate but also come out with grand prizes. I was a pride to the family. With this pride, came the loving support of my parents. Those were my joyful years of loving my dad too.

I never missed my dance classes until the day I started having my periods. Then, I was made to miss my dance classes for made-up reasons. I staged protests at home on why I was not allowed to dance anymore! Obviously, I was not attending the classes during my periods. What stopped me from going to the classes on other days? Dad was the one. I got to know from mom.

"My girl, come sit down. You are becoming big now," he said in a strange tone when I questioned him. "All our relatives and neighbours respect us, because of the decency we carry in public eyes. Whether it is our manners, our words, or our clothing. Look at your mom. Her sarees, handful of bangles, the big red bindi, and the neatly tied bun. Your dancing will grab a lot of attention on the clothes you wear. Dance is not for you anymore."

I then went to aggressive mode. I tried convincing him.

"Dance is my life. I want to learn as many dance forms as I can. I want to a major in dance, daddy. Please allow me to perform. The stage is made for me."

Dad got his chance of convincing me now.

"Bad eyes will be prying on you. Your body will change. You need to stay protected."

I did not quit questioning. "That is why you are there daddy. I am your daughter, and I know I am safe in your hands, and you will protect me. I do not know what dance has got to do with my safety?"

"Beta, the clothes they make you wear will be magnet to evil eyes. You have seen on TV na." *Wow, that was some nice reasoning there, dad.*

I had frowned. "Daddy, if you cannot support me, who else will?" My graph of emotions dropped from angry to pleading to begging.

I turned towards mom who was watching all this from the corner of the kitchen door.

"Mamma, please tell daddy. I cannot live without dance. Mamma, please!" Mom just stood there, sobbing. Dad had the final word.

"This is for your good, Beta. Listen to me." I stormed off towards my room, leaving a trail of sadness in the living area.

Soon, my mom dejectedly informed the dance teacher that I was no longer her student.

Knowing my dad's foul mouth when he gets angry, neither I nor my mom spoke another word about my dance from that day. So much for decency inside our home. While surrounded by others, dad would never use cuss words. Every time the radio played a song, my feet would be tapping to its rhythm.

Even when my mom sang devotional songs, my head would swing to the tunes. At night, I closed my eyes and drifted to sleep only after my ears were satisfied with five or more songs. Often, I would rise with the headphones still on, the playlist being ended during my dancing dreams. I woke up to the sound of emptiness, but each day, the shattering of my heart was ear-splitting. Eventually, I had come down to lying to my parents about my school programs too. Since they would not know, I sneakily enrolled in dance programs in school, but I would tell them that I was only participating in the singing functions. Because, according to my dear dad, singing was a decent art form for girls. The clothes are appropriate, and no guy can look at you in a way he should not.

Dad thought I would get over it in some time. That is how we kids were trained for. Over time, what remains is the life that our parents want us to lead, and our passions? well, they go to the remains. *Dear dad, this is not love to get over, this is my passion.* Passions never die. They might be buried or caged within us but when the time is right, they tend to rise like the phoenix. There was a way out (if you try to find one). My dance teacher had called my mom once.

She said, "Madam, your daughter has a bright future in dance. Please let her pursue it. If she gives up now, we would be losing a generation of dance tradition."

Mom was not the one who could decide on her own. For years, her decisions were snubbed. Now that I was growing up, according to my father, I offered options to mom. We discussed at length the best option to continue my dance classes. Within a few days of the arguments, convincing, crying, and whatnot with my mom, I rejoined my dance classes.

The dance classes were scheduled luckily according to school timings such that as soon as my school finished, I attended dance class too. Once I was back home, I would almost immediately practice too. I had one more hour to wind up my dance practice before dad came home. Within a few minutes of his arrival, my room would bore a studious look, payals safely locked until I call it again tomorrow. This had become a routine. Dad was happy that my studies were going well. I was happy that my dance classes were going well. He loved me for respecting his decision, but little did he know that my love was fading away for him.

Strange thing. As long as our parents support us in our talents, we love them. The love fizzes when they go against us. I should have had a bit more courage to confront dad. Since I was growing up, my decisions too mattered at home. I could have challenged him and convinced him. Dance was my love and so was he. But no, me being a coward, I hid. I could not let my passion meet his anger.

File 6: Towards Hope

My dance routines won many accolades, unknown to my father. But it is the proof of nature that anything hidden must eventually take a dramatic show out of the curtains. That was one such theatrical drama at home that day. I was chosen for a well-known dance competition which required me to travel to another city to compete. The college vacations were starting at the same time. Mom and I made excuses to dad saying we were off to our hometown for the entire stretch of vacation and will be meeting with relatives. It was a national-level show and will be aired on TV. Dad hardly ever showed interest in such shows, and we were quite sure we can get away with this. A parcel toppled the entire plan. Since I was competing in a big, national-level show, my dance teacher had ordered new payals that were delivered that Saturday. It was supposed to be a surprise for me. It came as a shock to my father. He received the parcel and opened it too! The payals sounded like music to me while my father fumed over it. Mom stood there, scared, unable to utter any word. I was ready to take on the fight. Any amount of convincing and justifying did not deter my father's decision. For him, girls only danced for the satisfaction of men. And he did not have room for such girls in his house.

I took the train alone. Mom was not allowed to step out. I was thrown out. Anyway, my luggage was packed and with it, I was packed off to a different city. Mom gave me some money and a spare phone. But that is about what I had when I left home, permanently. At the railway station, I sat on the pavement, still contemplating if I could go back home and forget about dancing. This little amount of money was not sufficient for a livelihood. And what about my stay? I had few relatives whom I could dial in. Since I had left home for good, I had to drop out of college. Without a degree at hand, my job opportunities looked bleak too. The track I had set on was an unknown and risky one. Unsure of any support, I had almost made up my mind to head back home, be sorry for my entire life and curse my dad for his behaviour at home. I swung around with such force that the payals fell on the ground. They did not just fall. They skated to a far distance. That was my dream calling. I was its parent. I could not orphan the payals. With it safely kept inside my bag, I had boarded the train, never to come back again. Life said it is going to be rugged. I said, bring it on!

My relatives were phoned by my father and strictly told not to entertain me in their house if at all I came banging on their door for help. I had a few old friends from school who had settled here, and they helped me to find a small apartment, enough to space my dancing legs. The competitions started soon. But first, I needed a survival kit. The first few days, I went job hunting to fend for myself. I found an 8 to 5 receptionist job in an IT company. Post 5 p.m., was full of dance practice. My dance teacher sent me her session videos that helped me to keep in connect. If not for my dance teacher, I would not be able to make ends meet. She often sent small sums of money even though I was earning some amount from my receptionist job. When I asked her why she sent me money, she would just coin the term "Shishya dakshina". As she was the only one not in touch with my family, she could be closer to me than my relatives. Hence, she also visited me sometimes and held workshops in my new city, so I could get her time and practice.

I breezed through most of the competitions laid for me. Making it to the top 20 at least was my first goal. I should have dreamt big subconsciously though. I had reached the top 10. The voting was open to the entire audience and nation now. Here was where I would know how well I have fared, and how much people will appreciate my art. I found out through the voting patterns that the audience too had a liking for my dance styles. I saw a few hoardings in the city that displayed my photo, with the voting number. This was all overwhelming for me. I knew I had built a fan base. Some of them even personally connected with me on social media handles. Many sent congratulatory messages. A few asked questions about myself. Many saw an inspirational figure in me. My dance teacher came to be well-known, back at my ex-city.

She video called one day, "You have been doing great dear! I knew your talent right from your childhood. I am glad it did not go a waste." After thanking her for staying put with me, we discussed at length my ongoing dance practices and the routines of the future.

There was still some kind of emptiness within me. The judges often asked the parents about their ward and their liking towards dance. In between dance performances, the other competitors would take their parents' blessings. I saw other contestants praising their parents for supporting them and likewise, the parents boasting their pride in their daughter or son. I usually kept to myself, sitting on the sofa, aloof. I stacked up all my emotions to put up a grand performance every time. When someone asked me about my parents, I would wander off to talk about my dance teacher instead. I often wondered if mom and dad were watching this show from their home. They better be proud of me. I had made it this far without anyone's help, except my dance teacher. Have I been dancing all this while to please the eyes of men, dad? I wanted to ask him this.

The top five had entered the final leg of the competition and one would be crowned the winner soon. The nights deprived me of my sleep. I wanted this badly. It was life-changing all the more now. More than the amount of winning and with it the fame, it had to do with me proving to my parents. Specifically, my dad's misconceptions on dance had to be drowned. My relatives were happy for me too but the fear of dad's hatred towards me made them stay away. They congratulated me over the phone. But the word never went out of their house. When their neighbours praised me, they praised me like any other person. Little did anyone know that I was related to them.

I left office at 5 p.m. as usual. Today, the practice was to be perfect. Even my dreams should dance to the song in unison. Tomorrow was the finals. I quickly grabbed a ready-to-mix food item from a nearby shop. Back at the apartment, I showered first. With freshness of the body, came the freshness of the mind too. I wore a white churidar. Tightening the knot of the red chunni around my waist, I bowed to Mother Earth and did the namaskar. I was ready to switch on the music that was planned for my finals when the phone rang.

Mom called me. Here is someone whose blessings will take me to victory.

I picked up the phone, elated. “Hi mom, how are you? Glad you called me. Tomorrow is my finals. Wish me luck! Thank you so much ma for calling. I really had hoped for your blessings. Hope you are seeing the show on TV? You saw that one episode where I did a fusion dance on your favorite song? Oh my god, the audience was roaring with claps. Well, I deserved the standing ovation for that! Ma, my dreams will come true if I win this. I can open my own dance school. I will bow to my art daily and live it in each breath. Isn’t it great?” I went on and on, without allowing her to blurt even one word. For many days, I missed sharing my success or hardships to anyone. Mom was the one before. After I left home, she too had distanced herself from me. This call was a much-needed breather. Finally, I get to talk to her and share all my feelings. At the other end, that was not the voice I anticipated though.

“You disgraceful girl!” dad had yelled. “If I had not meddled into your mother’s secret viewings of your dances, I would not have known what a shameful girl I gave birth to.

Your mother has been seeing the re-runs of your dance shows while I am away. I checkmated her today."

I was ready to hang up. This man will never comprehend the works of art. I was happy at least mom was silently rooting for me.

"You dance tomorrow, I will make your life hell. You have brought great sorrow to our family." He had hung up at the end of those words. I did not fully understand what he meant but this was monstrous. I cannot let anyone make my life a hell. I will let the heavens take me to a more peaceful adobe.

I crept up to the stage, late at night. I was still wearing my white clothes. My aerial act was the first to go tomorrow. A small light glowed on that prop, ready for its summon. The payals adorned my legs. I danced and danced to the fulfilment of my heart. Without music but with a rhythm of anger. When I was done dancing, I tied the chunni to the aerial prop. Yes, this was my final act. I stood up on the stool, and tied the chunni tightly to the prop. The stool let out a creaking sound. I balanced myself. All was set. Before letting the stool drop, one of my payals slithered to the floor. It journeyed down the stage, echoing before it dropped dead to silence after a few moments of withering. That is how I too packed off from this merciless life.

CHAPTER 9

Round is a Shape

Hello readers, I am Hope. It has been a while since I opened up to anyone about my past. Because I like to keep it there, in the past. It is worth exposing though. My past is the reason I was forced to consult a therapist and the reason why you have knocked on my file again. So, here I am, walking you through my past.

The past I refer to is not ages ago. It was only a few months back. I was in my last few semesters of college when my past ended. I was a little chubby and a healthy child since my inception in this world. I would like to call that. People called it fat. As kids, cuteness and being chubby are flattery. They go hand-in-hand. As age creeps on us, that protruding belly and what I termed as "healthy" translates to "unhealthy".

I was ragged through all my schooling days. I was not so thick-skinned to be positioned in a single desk in my school.

But I was made to sit alone, at the window corner of the classroom. It almost felt like I was distanced from the entire class. The teachers did not even turn towards my side during class while explaining the concepts. My seat was that far away. The only time the teacher sent daggering looks at me was when she wrote on the blackboard. That glare too was as quick as the blink of an eyelid. My mind used to tease me. What failed to make sense is why people looking at me were shamefaced when it should have been me. Younger kids in school would not express disgust or talk poorly about me. We have been taught to conduct well and respect everyone, right? And that was the only sane reason I was showered with glares.

The games period was hellish. The PT teacher did not like me. He purposefully made me run a few extra rounds around the ground.

"That needs a shape," he said sternly, looking at my belly. If I protested the extra running because I was too tired, my ass would get the beating from his stick.

Innocent as a child, I cried to his face, "Round is also a shape, sir."

He frowned. "Not when it sticks to your body. Four more rounds today."

It was only in my higher grades that I was cuffed by words.

"Hey bro, look at that belly. I hope I could use that to print a perfect round on my notebook." He made a swing of his palms to air-draw a round shape. I had just stood, with numbness packing over me. I went home to hide in my mom's pallu. Alas, I could not fit into that too. Strangely, in my mother's eyes, I was the intelligent one, a topper. Why was she the only one absorbing my positivity? Or was she internally hiding her sadness in her pallu? I wonder if her sorrow fitted in it. After a few rounds of paratha-eating, she would finally win over. Somehow her words made more sense. She helped me learn the method of switching on and off.

"Our mind is like the light switch. We have the ability to either allow light into the room or cloud it with darkness," she had consoled. "What you must do my child is, switch on that light to propel the knowledge transfer and switch it off when negativity tries to run over you."

She hoped I would follow this one day.

My classmates were preparing for a skit. I choose to walk out of the classroom and silently crept into the library. In few minutes, one of my classmates called out. I was elated. They had picked me for the skit! Hurriedly, I closed the book, handed it to the librarian and walked swiftly with my senior.

"Here, read the script and go through all the characters. Your name is bolded against your character's dialogues. Come on guys, let us get this going!" The house monitor ordered everyone.

Only, when I read the script, I knew why I was seen as fit. Instead of elation, I should have been cautious. It was the part of a fat landlord. Even though I had loved acting, I refused to do the role, merely out of fear of being mocked.

The house monitor tried his best to get me on board, saying, "Look, this is a good chance to revive. If people love your acting, they forget about appearances. People will love you for your work. Think about it."

I did not take that chance.

I did top with flying grades. Was it really flying? Because the weight of my loneliness pinched me to the ground more than my physical weight.

I was in college when the words hit like volcanoes. Here, there is nobody to stop you from talking (or rather ragging).

"Hey pumpkin, the day you find a girlfriend will be the day college will be doomed. But you never know! Love is blind, you see."

I did not hide under my mom's pallu now. Rather in my own room. Yes, the parathas helped that day too. I do not know what it was with my paratha fetish. They seemed to gobble all my sadness and placed them right where the whole problem arose from, my fat belly. Mom knew her switch on/off theory was not working for me. As in every engineering studies, theory is just worthless until put into implementation. This was when I went to the therapist. I needed someone impartial to guide me, to help me focus on my degree and more importantly, to use the switch on/off theory.

File 7: Towards Hope

I was into a few sessions with the therapist. Life was getting better. I liked the man. He used to motivate me like nobody ever did. He gave me advice that nobody ever did. He showed me a bright future like nobody ever did. I did not lose weight like he had once recommended. He had teased my mind once.

"Try changing your perspective. Why didn't you think of exercising to be healthy? Maybe they think you are unhealthy, rather than fat? Try changing your perspective, Hope."

His "maybes" were intimidating. It did direct me to think differently. I applied it, though in every other situation than this. It was taking time.

In one of the sessions, he tried a different method.

"You know, people who are hard-core diet freaks, also have a cheat day."

"What is a cheat day?" I had questioned.

"That is the day when there are no restrictions on eating any kind of food they want," he answered. "And that is why—a cheat day."

I had laughed. "I have no restrictions on any day. What do I cheat on?"

"We do the reverse in your case," he suggested. "You can eat whatever you want six days a week. One day is purely for dieting. Of having fruits, vegetables, and things that fall into the healthy platter."

This made sense. "Sounds like an idea! I will soon be on it."

It aligned to the switch on/off theory too. Nice.

"Which sport interests you?" he asked one day.

"I am not into any sports," I brushed him off. "Thanks to my PT teacher for keeping me away from that line of hobbies."

He did not push but he was clear. "Let us start with one sport. Shall we?"

I was implementing all that the therapist told me to do. But the belly was so huge that it needed a lot more than I was already doing. Shaping up was a different challenge. The current one was to first reduce the clobbered fat. For studying, to keep me focused, my stomach had to be full. Empty stomachs do not gather much knowledge. Empty stomachs also lead to frustration. Empty stomachs do not sleep well. With the stress of studies, came the craving for more food. While my intake was uploading exponentially, the diet, exercise, sports, and everything went downhill. The results did not show up due to my imbalanced habits.

It was during the farewell party of my seniors in college.

"Stop eating man! That will be good for you. Save the world, and leave some food for poor people. A lot are starving! Why don't you too?" my seniors commented or rather advised.

Really? Are you stupid? How can one live without eating? Did he intend to tell me that I was a waste to this already burdened earth? All these years, I had heard people mocking my body but never had anyone hit right at the problem, my eating habit. My mom's parathas are worth living for, I should have backfired him. Instead, I held the plate of food tight and stuffed myself more than necessary.

Now, my "maybes" started poking me. Maybe that guy was right. I had irregular eating patterns, cravings like a vulture and the capacity of a large boiler. Maybe that guy was right. If I stop eating for a while, my body will shape up a bit better. Maybe if I stopped being, everything would heal itself.

That was my last supper. Mom would be dejected if I did not eat the parathas before dying. I gobbled the parathas as much as my mouth could fill. I sat for a while for the food to digest and the thought of dying too. I placed the rat poison next to the empty plate. I sat hypnotised by the idea of dying. The idea had pounced on me like a cheetah and the more I looked at its eye, I knew death was the only solace. From then on, everything blurred, my mother's theory and my doctor's hope. As I picked up the rat poison with my trembling hands, a few drops spilled on the floor. Before I reached the tip of the bottle to my mouth, I saw a rat reaching its slow death. It took what, maybe a few minutes before it lay like a stone in front of me.

Without giving one more blink, I heard my mind say, "Let's be done with it." The suicide note prompted me to be quick. An empty poison bottle lay hushed on the table.

CHAPTER 10

Brainy but Penniless

Hello reader, I am Hopeless. The reason I introduce myself as Hopeless is because that is what I was called in my younger days. I was hopeless and penniless. I am an auto driver's child. You know these poor parents; they could not study themselves but keep high hopes for their children. My father was that. The only difference between me and the kids in my locality was that I wanted to study and many of them did not. Carrying the line of our parents' (or at least our father's) profession is perceived more proudly than pursuing what we like. As with every poor parent, my father was supportive of my studies. The only difference between him and the other parents was that he gave whatever he could to help in my studies and the other parents supported the kids by taking them to fields, making them do machinery work and kinds so their future is like their parents. I never rode an auto. By which I mean not in the driver's seat. My mode of transportation to school was auto and like other kids, my father dropped me.

The kids laughed the moment I stepped out of the auto. The school was a highly reputed one and suitable for the middle class and the rich, particularly spoilt kids. If I could make a small room for myself in this second home, it was because of my own merit and more importantly, my debating power. I used to participate in inter-school debating competitions which brought great prestige to my school. I loved school, apart from the gnawing eyes of my schoolmates. I was not a favourite among teachers either. I do not blame them, as I flew questions at them like it made them think whether they had really done their homework.

My father would advise, "Poverty is synonymous with sympathy. Education is synonymous with respect."

And throughout my life, these lines were imprinted on my heart like a permanent tattoo.

He explained further when I was young and didn't understand what it meant, "If we are poor, people will sympathise with us, maybe give us a little more money to sustain few days and forget us. People will pity us and walk away as though we wrote our fate at our birth. But, my child, education gives us power. It is only studies that can help us gain respect. Education is our permanent companion. Bringing home a culturally and knowledgably educated being also gives returns in the form of love and money. When there's an abundance of knowledge within us to show the world, then, they will forget the dryness of our caste and poverty line."

Had you ever imagined an uneducated man can make so much out of life? At least in this case, he did not need education to realise this, but experience.

With this little inspiration from home, I breezed through my years of schooling.

It was college time. This time I knew what to expect. I was like that typical "used-to" Indian. I expected people to ask about my caste, the area I came from, why I came in auto, etc. On the first day of college, for some reason, I did not feel like being an outsider. I was welcomed to the sight of boys wearing torn jeans and girls wearing shirts that were torn by part of their shoulders. Some boys had so much hair on top of their heads that a bird could nest in them. Girls did not wear bangles and neither kept *bindi*. I felt so bad for them. I was poor but not so poor that my father couldn't afford me a well-knit cloth. He got me a variety of bangles. My brother too didn't have holes in his clothes. Only later during the interactions with my college mates did I come to know that these were the trending fashion styles these days.

For once in my life, I woke up to a relationship called friends. Friendship is like a dew drop. The dew does not go in search of plants. It plants itself in comfortable leaves. The beauty of it is that, whether it be a small grass or a tall tree, friendship does not bifurcate between the two.

I was not surprised at the number of friends I made in college. The number was huge. Even after graduation, nobody knew that this poor girl had made it through the crucial years of her life by what she did best—study. On the graduation day, among the bustling crowd, stood an auto far away, shining, and bright, proudly representing its child. You would bet on its future also going to be shining and bright, right?

File 8: Towards Hope

Job postings had commenced. I cleared the aptitude tests with no hurdles. My instincts had told me I would have the option to choose the company I would work for. And I did settle for a reputed one. I was the first one in my poverty-stricken locality to taste the work of an IT company. The money was good and the job was perfect. It fed my family well. In all my years of growing up, there was one thing that had not budged with time: my father and his persistence. Even then, I travelled to office by his auto. For a few days, it went unnoticed. But the prying eyes of gossip mongers never get satisfied by mere viewing. They will go all out to extract personal details.

Office, I realised, was like a second home. We spend as much time in here as at our homes. And at some point, we are bound to connect personally with our team-mates. Many such occasions came where my personal life was discussed. I could not shy away and neither did I feel comfortable giving much details. Slowly, my entire life peeled in front of them. They knew my address, my caste, my father's job, and my societal status. Maybe they should have taken me as an inspiration, no? My life was not any less than a miracle with sprinkles of luck and large portions of hard work.

"Hey, you auto girl, I wonder how you got into this company. Did you drive the auto before someone accidentally put you on this job?"

Yes, I was made fun of throughout my life. Never had anyone ever chastised my father's profession. It was downhill for me. My performance sucked. I was not working to my full potential. I laid at the mercy of my colleagues, wishing every day, that today, it will stop. That today, I can concentrate on work. That today, I wish my merit spoke.

On one rainy day, I sat unusually quiet in the auto. My father knew I was not okay in this job. Any parameter of consoling did not give any output. I went too deep into my own thoughts, tangled between one insult to the other, unable to get out. He drove me home like this almost every day until I had crashed into a deep slumber, or did I just fall into my own pitiful pit? I jolted out of my inner world as suddenly as my father had stopped the auto. An old man was drenched from top to bottom. My father asked him if he could drop him home. Thinking I was already a passenger, he hesitated to board.

Father, sensing his dilemma, had said, "Sir, she is my daughter. We are going back home. I shall drop you. Please come."

It was then that he came with us. That ride changed my life.

I could not remember what I had said to him. He had given me an address to meet him at the earliest. I did not know why I came here. I had no clue what of he said about himself. Steadily, as the sessions were progressing, the therapist came into my forgotten memory. That was him, in the auto that night. Apparently, my father had spoken all about my unfortunate situation. That is when he had given his card for visiting. He never took fees from me.

When I enquired why, he said, "One day, you will definitely bring me your fees. Not now. I pity you. Not until you appreciate yourself. Have you ever thought of your own worth? Maybe, this job is not worthy of you? For how long can you keep away from people? They are here to speak like you do. Accept the truth and get on with your life."

Dear therapist, I took this job because I liked it and because I was worth it. How dare you point fingers at my job? I have not reached this height to hear words of unworthiness. Do you also think I am hopeless? That was my introduction into this world anyway. I am going to throw your fees on your face as soon as possible. You are no better than anybody, just sympathising and doing nothing. I debated all this in my head. But out came nothing. He pinched me with the same principles I lived by. If I held by my "for," he went "against" it. Why was he even debating with me? Wasn't he supposed to get me out of this? Did he forget that I was a debate champion? He was no match for my skills.

For many reasons, I just could not understand the doctor and neither the purpose of my life. If I had not been a burden to my parents, they would have lived happily ever after. That is right, after I have left this world. This was just a step. There is a huge stair ahead to cover, my job, my marriage, and what not baggage that a child comes with. Better go away when the time is right. Things will settle as they should with the worry of one person less. Anyway, the therapist was not of much help either. I was not anywhere near happy. Let us end this with where it all started—being born an auto driver's child. If there is anything like rebirth, then I pray to be born rich.

It was pitch dark on the highway. There would be many vehicles passing by. This suicide would be easy. I walked for a long time, still contemplating suicide. I heard a screeching noise a few meters ahead of me. Definitely it was the truck which sped away. A poor little kitten bore the death of speeding. It took few breaths before it lay still. Hmmm, that was swift. Mine would be too. I drank a cup of coffee so I did not doze off. I wanted to witness my own death. I stood in the middle of the road, already like a ghost. A distant auto sound pierced my ears and then came the truck which blurred every other sound. I finally closed my eyes as the truck approached nearer. It was only a matter of a few minutes before I would never open my eyes. I just hoped the truck was fast enough to kill me rather than crippling me for my entire life.

CHAPTER 11

Birth of Social Media

Naveen was in Hawaii. He seemed to be having a gala time with his friends.

Mitra graduated from a foreign institute. The graduation hat was intimidating.

Krishna got married. To his childhood love. I could not help but notice the tattoos on each of their hands with their names.

Shakti sky dived. She was always the daring kind anyways.

Varun had got a long-term opportunity in the US. Long wait after all.

Mythili and her husband were celebrating their fifth anniversary. The lovey-dovey types who post everything about their whereabouts and important dates.

Poonam boasted about how great a mother she is. Ha! Typical mother.

Deepti posted one with her young child. She had lost her pregnancy curves.

Vignesh and Sannidhi were out for a date night. No special occasion. Just spending quality time.

Hi, I am Hope, posts zero, photos zero, happiness zero.

When the therapist showed me this page in my file, I was overwhelmed at the pace with which he made a point to note everything I had muttered, of course, in a state of depression. Not mincing even a single word that I spluttered with so much jealousy. Do you think I was elated while telling the above to my therapist? Never. In each session, he diligently illustrated each emotion in his notes.

Every session he would show me this page and ask me, "Today, what did you tell me about yourself?" Not one note of his had my name or my problems in it.

When he enquired with seriousness, "Why did you come to me, Hope? What is your problem?"

"I do not know what my problem is," I replied critically. "I want you to find it."

You bet he found it, encrypted in all my sessions. My diagnosis, in the words of the doctor, read as follows: "Mother of a 3-year-old child. Craves for attention from others and time from her family. Finds others' lives as being happier than hers. Tint of jealously but a high level of self-pity. Looks down upon herself. Lost herself. Suffering from acute social media depression. No visible improvement from previous sessions."

Yes, he summed it up perfectly. After the birth of my child, following a few traditions, I could not do much work at home except to take care of my child. You know, these babies, they sleep a lot more than playing in their initial years. And that lead to me having a lot of time by myself. What could I have done right? I could read a good book. I could inculcate a new hobby. I could tend to my child's cleanliness. I could learn new lullabies. I could give a helping hand to my mother. Worst, I could even sleep along with my child and get the much-needed post-pregnancy rest. But what did I do? I fell into the addiction of spying on others' lives and what better place to do it than on social media? I had all kinds of accounts: Facebook, Instagram, Twitter, and many more that I cannot count. You name it, I had it.

Just so you know, I was not on any dating app, only the places where people did not need a left or right swipe. They were all over your feed. It bit me like a bug. The more I tried to avoid it, the more it scratched the wound. As a mother fresh out of the brewery, I wanted sympathy from others, yearned for special treatment, longed for a day off without the child, and felt insufficiency in being loved. My idle mind was devilish, alright, as is the famous saying. When I saw others bragging about their perfect lives, I could not help but re-look at my own life and wonder what a mess I was in. But really, instead of cleaning it up, I messed it up even more. My mind was like that hostel guy whose room piled up with more unclean clothes than dirt. Subconsciously, I did know what was happening to me. Something held me from bringing out that good part of me. I did not know what force it was. Maybe that is what the physics of depression is.

After giving it a lot of thought, I decided to see a counsellor. My therapist was the most patient person I had ever known. He took time. The sessions were short but insightful.

Every session, he fed me with only one thought, "You are looking at it wrong and thinking about it wrong."

What does this mean? Never mind, I did not understand either. I went along and kept this statement in the warehouse of some intricate part of my mind. He hoped, just one day, some day, I would be smart enough to think this through.

File 9: Towards Hope

My baby was growing just fine. I was a good mother as every mother thinks the same. Unfortunately, the acknowledgements do not come from close people. It is with a self-consoling machine that we mothers must self-appreciate.

I started work again and was engrossed in better things in life. My priorities had changed. Life was happening. The doctor was partly a witness to this change. The pimple that had harboured at the coast of my early pregnancies did not disappear though. It was expanding. I was still addicted. Every now and then my fingers would itch if I did not check my phone. Specifically, the posts by my friends. I wondered if my friends would think of me as a friend if they knew I actually kept a bad eye on them.

That one day, it was one post that toppled my mind blindly. One of my Facebook friends, not a close one, but still a friend since it is tagged like that on Facebook, had recently delivered a baby. Within a few months, I could see her beautiful curves again, her skin glowing. I faced myself in the mirror that night.

"Look at you," I had said to myself, "Have you seen your belly? Did you do the exercise as promised to yourself? Have you thought of taking care of yourself first? Look at your curves, going haywire all over the body. Not one part of the body is in the right proportion. The skin is wrinkling already! Open your wardrobe. Piles of fading dresses lie there. What have you done to yourself?"

I hated myself that day. I did not speak out loud but the mirror spoke a lot.

My social media handles were empty under my own profile. I had posted nothing. What was there to post anyway? I was not vacationing, hadn't become fat to fit in one frame of the photo, life's routine had set in with the child and nothing was happening. That night, I could not sleep and felt wasted. In the wee hours, before the sun peeped through my bedroom window, I finished writing the suicide note. On all my social media handles. I kept it in draft mode, took a quick bath, and dressed pretty. For my final journey. Today, somebody would finally see my post. They will regret not sympathising with me.

Their guilt will chew them, thinking—someday, I should have asked her, "How are you doing?" Today, they will remember a friend long forgotten in their busy lives. Today, they will know how much hurt they engraved in my heart. Today, they will realise, maybe their happiness is somebody else's food for depression. In all their posts of their lives, there is somebody else wishing it could be theirs.

If only you had asked, "Are you fine?"

If only you had asked, "Can we meet over a cup of coffee?"

If only you had asked, "How's life been?"

If only you had asked all these questions, I would have happily given answers and probably not have been addicted to spying on you. I needed your time, your love. But all of you spent it on social media. I saw the time you spent there. I saw the love you poured into others over there. Haven't you had enough of the buzz of life on social media? Isn't anything personal now? That is exactly what I was looking for, dear social media friends. I did not care about the likes, neither the comments. I wanted a personal interaction to tell you how I have been in life.

I stepped in front of the mirror.

"Am I not looking beautiful today?" I asked sarcastically.

"I pity the inner beauty that you hide so well to outshine your outer beauty. You are looking at it wrong and thinking about it wrong," the mirror replied back calmly.

"Wait, what did you just say? Looking at it wrong and thinking about it wrong? Wow, what a lovely quote. I really do not have time for thinking anything now. Gotta go to a better world."

The different tabs of the laptop had my social handles on them. Each one proudly showcasing my masterpiece: the suicide note. As I click "post" on each of these, I will be done and dusted. Done with this life and reduced to dust.

CHAPTER 12

Strange Invitations

After an interesting eleven days of story-reading, I feasted on all the Hope files of Pappa. It was indeed grueling. I could hear a drum-roll from my mind. The stories might have been short but like Pappa always said, I had to put in my emotion for every sentence.

"If you cannot emotionally connect to their problems, you will never be able to commiserate. And hence, you will not donate the right solution," he often clarified.

I rang up Priya. Finally, I could be at her disposal. Due to the incapacitating files, I had lost count of the days left for our wedding. The number was busy. Understandable. I waited to hear back from her.

I closed the last of the files and made a hot cup of tea for myself. Or was it coffee? I cannot remember as I was still reeling because of these eleven lives, repeatedly in a trance. I tiptoed to the balcony. I sat on the rocking chair, cross-legged, sipping the tea or whatever, just thinking for as long as the clock ticked to the dark side of the day. Night fell as the sun escaped to another place, promising a fresh start. But the files did not decamp my trip to them. I let all of them take me on a trek to their peaks, wondering about the journey they stepped into called life. The question is, had they ever lived it to fulfilment? Had they given up on the cake?

This world has people, each day, being criticised for their very existence. And these are only eleven such troubled beings. I could not even start to imagine the population that goes through these feelings every day, silently, building a draconic world of their own inside them. There is a fine visible line between being a critic and an opinion-giver. More often, the former engulfs the well-wisher. While being an open-minded critic is good, the irritability factor rises when the blows come too often, almost every other day. The marathon of patience runs out one day, tired of the pain and puffing out all the anger. Before it even reaches the finish line, the plan of a drastic step is sketched in the mind. It just needs one trigger to crumble the life we led. Just one trigger. Trigger. I shook my head vigorously to erase that last part. It painted a different scenery.

I walked back to the kitchen and washed the cup of tea. *Gosh, what did I drink?* I laid my head on the sofa pillow, one hand above my head. I gazed at the beautifully painted wall ahead, still visualising the files. Nevertheless, these Hope files were dead, I concluded suddenly. I would have preferred if Pappa called them suicide files rather than Hope files. This also meant that Pappa was not a good therapist. If you cannot save your customers from disgrace, what kind of a service provider are you? I knew Pappa was a good advocate, as I received a few pointers myself occasionally. Oh well, maybe these were the only cases in which he failed. There could be many other files buried in his shelf that were successfully treated out of their misery.

Some kind of magic led me back to the study room. I looked at the faces of the files, calling me again. Just then, Priya called.

"Hey!" I picked up the phone.

"Where have you been, darling?" checked Priya.

"You won't believe it! I went through the files. All of them. Great stories. But what is the use if they could never deal with their so-called problems? How do you read books like these? Every book has to have a happy ending!" I filled her in on the details and also debated. I heard a low sigh from Priya before she spoke.

"Not all stories have a happy ending. And they are not stories. They are people. People have problems, dear. That is the way of life. Some can deal with it. Some cannot. Not all. You and I had Pappa backing us all the time! Not everyone does, do they?"

"Yeah, maybe," I answered thoughtfully after a long pause, standing up. Priya quickly changed the topic.

"So, my dear, now that the files have given you enough, could you please spare time for our first and last wedding? I have lots going on and really need your help. The wedding is just three days away!"

"Three days? Wow. I am sorry Priya for not thinking about us. I will report to you tomorrow, captain!" I saluted.

"At least I am glad that you never gave up on reading the files, unlike the other books I gave you." Priya heard the continuous beeps on the phone just as she was concluding her, "I love you."

I had cut the call when I heard a part of her last sentence more clearly than ever. I read that text again on the glaring files.

NEVER GIVE UP

A

This must be a clue. My mind was speeding now. It was probably the detective hat again. I did not really like putting my mind to work a lot. I liked to keep it stress-free. This was literally killing me. The mystery of the files was deepening. If the handwriting on the letters was the same, it also meant that the same person wrote them, which also meant that they scratched the "I" and wrote the "A." They read it as "NEVER GIVE UP" to "NEVER GAVE UP." Doesn't it mean they did not give up hope and are still alive? But how would I know? The names were not on the files!

Though there were no mention of the names of the patients, each of the file had their addresses. Now, there was only one way to find out about these "Hopes".

* * *

I was three days away from my wedding day. I hurriedly placed the invites into each of the envelopes. I made sure I bolded Pappa's name on the top of the invite so that the person identifies immediately. I even took the effort to reword the entire invitation as though Pappa is inviting them for his son's wedding.

Honestly, I did not know what to expect out of this act. Was I hoping for them to turn up? Will some family member of theirs come and crash my wedding? Because Pappa had failed to cure them. Maybe there was nobody at the address now. Are they dead, just like the files? Probably they have met Pappa upstairs in heaven? Or hell, for they went against a life given by God? Who knows what deeds count as heaven-friendly or hell-friendly?

The mind plays well, again. Assumptions are the kings of misunderstandings. I shook off these questions for now and saved all the stress for the wedding. I went back to my wedding preparations, leaving these assumptions to reveal their truth on the wedding day. In three days, the Hope files would remove the darkness in me about Pappa's death.

My heart felt heavy again, unable to take the weight of the wait. Ha! A little funny there.

I quietly questioned Pappa, "What do you have in store for me?" I knew Pappa was around. His soul was still lingering.

I gave a hundred percent of my mind and heart to Priya for the big day.

CHAPTER 13

A Lot's in a Name

Priya was aware of my plight. For three days, she constantly tried to deviate me away from other distractions, especially regarding Pappa's files. We had a lot of work to do, ourselves, for the wedding. It was a special day for us, and Priya made sure nothing was going to come in between these pompous celebrations. She did well in handling both me and the preparations!

Finally, the day arrived. Priya and I were bound by the sacred thread and the chants of promises of a lifelong companionship.

The wedding was followed by the reception on the same day. My special guests had not arrived yet. Consciously, I was hoping the Hopes came in. The possibility of those being real suicide stories scored higher. Slowly, as I came to terms with this very thought, the files faded out of my memory. Yes, they needed some salvation from my pondering. I would set them free from my mind, never to return to their files again. They were long gone, anyway, physically from this world. It was their soul that was to be freed from my mind.

The guests whizzed past me, while I was freeing the captivated Hope files. The guests were a blur to my vision. I shook their hands, standing dazed. When the photos print out, I would see myself in a transfixed state for a certain period on my reception day. The plastic smile and the uninterested face would give away my disturbed state. Priya will be angry. I will have to prepare a good explanation.

The guests were nearly emptying the hall. Out of the almost clear field, my sight cleared too. I could see them, finally. The nine players stood right in front of me. Did I smile for the first time for the camera whole-heartedly? Priya would know. I was still in a trance but a good one. I turned to Priya, not sure how to contain my excitement. She held my hand, gave a little pat on it, which conveyed, "You did it!"

They all were alive! I now felt the jitters, not of the wedding but of all the Hopes being in one piece, physically, together. A gloomy burden dropped from my heart, feeling elated that after all, Pappa was not a dud. Also, I owe myself a slap for thinking he could be one.

Alive. Hope. Never gave up.

* * *

Each one of them introduced themselves to Priya and me. Because their eyes were eagerly searching for their savior, my Pappa, I had to give them the sad news.

"Dad is no more. I wondered what was special about you all that you guys needed a separate shelf in dad's office. With no time to waste, and the curiosity getting the worst side of me, I decided to send out the invitations to you. Honestly, if dad would have been with us, he would be proud of all of us," I spoke in a rush.

The old man's eyes watered instantaneously.

Within a few more minutes, each of us had briefly introduced ourselves. Luckily, these guys were the last guests to our reception party and this one enigmatic photo was worth a click.

We stood on the podium in a straight horizontal line, so the photographer could get the perfect shot of the survivors. As is the habitual ritual, he tried aligning us. While he was still struggling to get us into one frame, I swept my eyes from one corner to the other. Now that I knew all their names, something made sense.

"Ok sir, ready?" shouted the photographer with a thumbs up.

Hurriedly, I replied, "No, wait!"

Priya must have sensed I caught something. "What's going on?" she asked.

I started forming the line. I took each one by their shoulder and placed them accordingly. With glittering eyes, I called up Priya, facing them.

She stood stoked. As the guys stood for the photo, this is what the first letter of their names read—

E V E R G A V E U

Priya and I smiled at each other. Retracting our steps for the photo, we completed the puzzle.

I stood, now at the first and Priya at the last end of the queue.

We now read—

N E V E R G A V E U P

Hi, I am Nithin. I am one of the Hopes.

Hi, I am Priya. I too am one of the Hopes.

That makes eleven Hope files.

The smile I had for this one photo, were like a million beautiful stars loved by the handsome night.

CHAPTER 14

A Hairy Situation

As you have come to know now, I am Nithin, a Hope. My Pappa was a therapist. Never would I have thought that I would be one of my own dad's Hope files. But, yes, here I am. And it is time to tell my own survival story.

Girls fell for my looks, right from my school days. Fairly tall, fleshed physique, charm in the smile, and a great styling personality. That was me. Although I welcomed all the attention, I did not act smart towards anybody. I was a friend to everyone, in the same way. No partialities. And that goes for girls too. I was not the one who proposed to girls, and believe it or not, I was not anyone's proposal preference either. They liked me for who I was, and that mostly counted as a trustful friend.

I would prefer considering most people as my acquaintances and only a handful of them as my friends. A friend would know you in and out. Mainly your inner pain and your outer pretention.

After my mom's untimely death, a few people always stood by me. I hung out with them frequently. Planned weekend getaways were a thing. Our gang loved trekking, long biking rides, and seldom a comfort drinking session on the beach. Travel made me a better person. Travel was a mind-soothing exercise. Travel was being a limited-period *Ghajini*. In my journeys of exploration of myself, I had another conscious and protective soul with me—my friends.

There was one more, dear friend of mine, back at home, Pappa. He altered like a chameleon during my growing years. After mom left us, he became a split personality, sometimes scolding like mom and most times, being the dad he was. Gradually, he mimicked the role of a friend.

Surrounding me, there was always love, kindness, and laughter. I was living in a perfect world of dreams. Well, life is a perfect concoction of imperfections. This is something we grasp only when we drink it.

During my early twenties, I started balding. I gave a damn.

I twisted Shakespeare's famous quote to "What's in a hair (instead of the name)?"

Life happens and when situations circulate, friends are the ones who will also always stand by. They said, handsomeness was still a part of me. Who says physical looks must be coined as handsome? I can be romantically handsome. I can be intelligently handsome. I can be handsome in many ways. I celebrated this famous twisted quote of mine, until my marriages alliances showed up. Apparently, the groom must have hairs on his head, that too, well-flourished. I said, I was balding and not yet fully-bald. But no, hair matters.

I remember one pushy parent. So, this one parent was okay to the alliance if I wore a wig. The photos came nicely. All relatives were happy. The girl could boast of our selfies. Yes, she told me this on our one-on-one. Pappa had looked uncertainly towards me after the end of all discussions.

I gritted my teeth right towards the girl's dad and politely asked, "Are you going to give hair colours as dowry for my wig? Because you see, I will get old and I would like your people to notice that on my hair too."

Pappa said I was rude to them as they barged out of the house.

Oh, there was another alliance. Sensible guys though. At least they came up with practical solutions. They agreed to completely cover my head with the turban on the marriage day. But there would be no reception. Think about it, how would they cover my head in reception? My dad was a little apprehensive of this condition. Anyway, he looked towards me for a hint.

I hovered tall in the hall, facing the girl's father, politely asking, "How do you plan to cover my tummy? I am a tad bit fat too."

Pappa said I was rude to them too as they barged out of the house.

Then one other family had a permanent solution to this non-existent problem. Hair gone, marriage on! The war was on. The plan was laid out in front of me. I would travel all the way from Delhi to Tirupati. I sacrifice my whatever-is-left hair to God. He blesses me for this sacrifice. I come back to Delhi and get married. They would praise this sacrificial lamb in front of their relatives.

"My son-in-law vowed that whenever he would get a lucky girl, he would shave off his head and offer the same to God."

Wow, this guy came up with a lot of praises for me though or well, for his daughter indirectly. Only if I went completely bald. My dad shook his head, and before he turned towards me, I was already on my feet this time.

"Uncle, I cannot live a life which somebody else will dictate. I cannot change for society."

Pappa said I was polite to them.

These are a few instances of me either being rude or politely declining the alliance. The truth was, I had grown tired of the steady convincing.

File 10: Towards Hope

I pleaded Pappa to stop the alliance searching. He obliged my pain. However, he frequently checked on my health—mental state mainly. He was more interested in the friend group I had. He constantly questioned my trip details off late. On a lazy weekend, he raised a lingering question.

"Do you have friends who are girls? What is the bond with them like? Have you liked any girl in particular?"

"Pappa, that's too many questions for a single context," I cut him short. A quick laugh left our mouths.

Pappa sat on the chair, looking far ahead but waiting for my reply.

Sensing his curiosity, I had replied, "You know how I am with girls. I am a charmer, Pappa."

Pappa rolled his eyes. "And nobody has fallen for it yet?"

"Those girls are my friends," I continued. "I treat them the same as my guy gang. No special treatment to anybody specifically. They do come on trips. They are as much fun as any of my other friends. That's about it." Convinced by my own answer, I leaned back on my chair, joining my hands behind my head.

A long silence dangled in the air. Detective Pappa didn't give up.

"Still, is there any girl with whom you share everything? I mean, about your life, career, future, or even just sharing a bad day?"

That chair was not meant for me to rest on, I had thought. I placed my elbows on my thighs and leaned front to firmly answer him.

"Pappa, my friends know everything about me. Be it a guy or a girl, we all share the pain and happiness of everyone."

I stood up to leave the room, signalling an end to this conversation.

* * *

I started avoiding Pappa in the coming days. His questions were pricking me even more. My friends were tired of my constant nagging too. Apart from our life that we share with friends, we often forget that we all have an individual life too. It is important to draw a line between these two lives. Each one of us, knowingly, is struggling with a problem at the granularity level, unknown to the world outside. I purposefully missed the gang trips. I absconded for days, on a solo trip. The mind can be devilish sometimes when alone. The devil does not know how to divert from the realm of recurrent suicidal thoughts. That is the job of angels that come in the form of friends. Unfortunately, I stayed with the devil rather than embracing my angels.

For one of the trips, my friends forced me to join them. It was a long time since I went on trips with the gang. It was a trekking spot. The devil had a strong hold of me then. I had informed Pappa about the trek the previous night with a lot of enthusiasm. Pappa was happy to see me happy about this trip. He thought, maybe I was getting better. He slept peacefully that night probably. Little did he know how peacefully I planned to sleep the next day. I tip-toed to Pappa's room in the dead-night, opened a drawer next to his bed. He was fast asleep, letting out a soft snore. I snuck the pistol in my bag, kissed my dad on his forehead, and left for the last leg of my journey. The devil was happy. Angels did not know what is to come.

We drove to a small shack in the wee hours of morning, at the foot of the hill which we planned to trek. My friends were smoking the hot tea in the fog covered road-side vendor shop. I excused myself for a pee and left the spot. I walked for a long time until I escaped the bare eyes of my friends. Anyway, the fog added to the advantage to the crime I was about to commit. The trees ruffled softly, there was an eerie silence and the only shout that could be heard will be that of my pistol's bullet. The remainder of my hair had made space for the trigger. I held the pistol on my forehead, right where my problem was. I had finally remembered all those who had made my life a beautiful journey till today. My dad and friends had played a pivotal role. The trees could hear the "Sorry" I breathed out to my well-wishers. I had been ready for my peaceful sleep.

I could envision mom with my closed eyes. I would finally sleep on her lap. As I pulled the trigger, she reminded me of a promise she had asked for.

"Nithin, promise me that you will take care of Pappa, always, until his last breath."

I opened my eyes to this realisation. She left me as fast as she had come to me and took the devil away from me. At the same time, one of my friends held my hand to plummet the bullet to the forehead of high-rising trees rather than the forehead of the low-rising hairs of mine. My angel had saved me.

Little did I know that dad was brewing my own Hope file in his office.

Hi once again, I am Nithin. I survived a life. I survived for another loved one's life.

CHAPTER 15

Dark Chocolate

Hi, I am Priya, now Nithin's wife. I am a Hope file too. I was the most loved Hope of Nithin's dad. He liked me for the maturity of my thinking. And how do I know I was his most loved patient, you ask?

He told me once, "Priya, if there comes a day to cry for somebody else's pain, it would be you. You are more like a family to me rather than a patient. I don't expect a smart one like you to disappoint me."

In the other cases I think, mostly, people have personally visited Nithin's dad. In my scenario though, he was the one to visit me, initially, of course. The mess I had made myself of was worth a therapist's visit though. Here is my issue in a gist—

Darkness surrounded me, and within me.

Even when the Sun shone brightly, darkness still kissed me.

Even the dark chocolate prided with its colour.

I could not ask for a better mirror than the school's blackboard.

Well, it is now that even the schools have a fairer sex, the white board.

I could walk in the scary night, and still get unnoticed.

It is the darkness of your heart that does not see the light in me.

If you have not guessed already, I am a dark-skinned girl. I was a subset of the holy matrimony of my dark birthparents. Obviously, if I were a tone lighter than them, it would be a disgrace to God's work of creation.

I pretty much summed up my life in the poem above. My parents gave me the best education and culture that one could get. They gave me the best of skin colour too. Thankfully, the education system was not biased on anyone's physical appearance. It moulded one's strengthening of knowledge alone. That is partially a problem. No education system can prepare us for life. It can only support our monetary benefits of life, but not of any hurdles.

In school and colleges, it was not only me with a dark skin. I had company. That proved as some relief as the mind is trained to accept a fault if it is not only us who has committed it. Office was a professional environment where I was lauded for my work. What was wonderful about the school, colleges and offices was, they are a temporary part of your life. But your birth itself is questioned when you must become a permanent part of somebody's life. My marriage alliances were no different than what Nithin laid out in his story. Been there, experienced the same. Funnily, all my alliances were of dark-toned boys too. But dark-toned boys are marked as handsome, you see. He needs a fair girl to complement him. Make-up artists can put in effort to make the girl a tad bit fairer for the wedding at least. But that was just the face area. What about other parts of the body? There was also a risk of uncovering my actual skin colour when meeting relatives. There were numerous pretentions to reject my alliance. And I blamed no one. If some prince charming is designed for us, he will have to accept the way I am designed too. And thus, my mind was made. Unfortunately, parents do not grasp this.

There was one difference between Nithin and me in how we dealt with the rejections. He succumbed to internal aggression building, while I patiently waited for my prince charming. No guesses now to know who that charmer was! We both were two sides of the coin. One a fire and the other one ice. Nithin was suicidal and I was not. Then why was I a patient to Nithin's dad, you ask?

File 11: Towards Hope

The alliances were taking a toll on not only myself but my parents too. Unlike Nithin's dad, my parents would not stop the train of alliances. With all the educational qualifications and working in an MNC, I was still a burden on my parents.

Clearly, I had told them that the finances of my marriage will be funded from my own pocket. Alas, it fell on conservative ears. We were like the normal middle-class family that held religious values at the mountain level and forgot basic human values at the ant level.

I had tried moving out of the town. Mom had objected to it, fearing for any kind of untoward incident.

"It's no better here, mom. There is not one guy who can accept me as a life partner. Do you think a stranger will even look at me as a rape target? Forget it. Destiny will choose what's good to come," I had consoled her. No amount of pestering was dithering her searching.

"Beta, we cannot sit at home and expect your prince to fall on your lap. Searching will give us some hope," she had quipped.

Frustrated, I had answered, "Hope and patience go together mom. You cannot be looking for a guy like this. Everything will fall in place. Give it some time."

"We have a responsibility and that's you. Girls cannot be unmarried for too long. People are already gossiping," she used to hit back.

I had made a decision though.

"Mom, one month from now, your responsibility will be over. I have got a job in Delhi and I am moving out. It is a contract for two years, and then I will be back home. We can try again later."

Mom stood with an angry face, surprised at her daughter making lightning-fast decisions.

"Talk to your dad," she had shouted as I barged out of the room. "Maybe he can put some sense in you."

I had shifted to Delhi within two weeks on the pretext of finding accommodation and settling down before I reported to work. These two weeks, the house hosted a gloomy silence all the time. I was talking to neither of my parents. While they debated who will talk to me every day, I looked for an escapade. Family dinners became rare. I somehow stayed put for two weeks and off I went to another town, away from the marriage pressure. I set on a career enhancement plan. The mind needed a place to work properly and it was definitely not happening with my parents.

I spoke to mom once a week and never with dad. All those childhood years of love had reduced to a mere load on my parents. It was hard talking to mom for one day too. She never asked me how my job was, how I spent my weekends, or what was I cooking that day. All she had to talk about was my marriage and how I have deprived dad of a proud daughter, just because marriage was not happening, I became the devil now. Over a period, I just heard her, and stopped reacting to anything that was said.

A year passed by, with me being happy with my life. But life isn't a fair play, is it? Where there is an abundance of happiness, a little sorrow is meant to be. It was 2:30 a.m. when the phone rang. Startled and still rubbing my sleep off, I picked mom's call.

"Hello mom. What makes you call me at this time? I do not want to talk about any marriage."

I had heard a sob and then her voice came clearly, "Your dad has breathed his last. Please come over."

I had took the next available flight. I was in a state undiscovered by myself, walking from the airport to my home. The outside surrounding had shut off from my systems and all that seemed replaying was my childhood. I came home to a sea of people, swarmed around my home. I frantically searched for mom when my neighbour aunty rushed towards me.

"Aunty, where is mom?" I shook her shoulder then to get something out of her uncontrollable crying.

* * *

All the rituals were done. I sat at a small podium right in front of our home's door. The tears streamed downwards. In a single day, I became an orphan. The guilt crushed me. Along with dad, mom had been called too, to a better place. Now, this is where I became suicidal. The burden of my skin colour had not smitten me as much as the guilt of leaving my parents unattended did. I had a choice to stay back at home. My career and the happiness of my lonely life blinded me of the fact that my parents were suffering each day. They always had me in their mind. Slowly, like a bacterium, the burden had eaten them from within. Dad was never on my call list. And I had withdrawn from mom too.

I quit my job at Delhi. I had left home with a lot of courage and sparkle of a new life in a different city. That day, the suitcases held a baggage of guilt. The sparkle in the eye flowed as tears. I came back, alone, to my home sweet home. Only, it was not a filled home. The dust settled very soon on the furniture. The curtains never opened to the sun. My clothes were always dancing on the floor. The bedroom was always occupied by me. I let my guilt fill my globe. My home kind of bore a haunted look now, in which lived a breathing ghost. That was my problem, I was still breathing.

The servant came home every day. I know this because I never walked up to open the door. I loved my loneliness. Sometimes, in the dead of the night, I would step out to grab dinner. Once the night's sickness wore out, I would walk back home and fall asleep. When the servant rang the bell every morning, I just did not do anything. Well, she had not given up either.

It was one such night when I had strolled out that I chanced upon Nithin's dad. I had sat at a roadside hotel, sipping a hot tea, waiting for my dinner when he drove past. I can say it was late in the night as he was worried and offered to drop me home. I did not answer to any of his questions. I sat in his car, put on a google map on my phone and let him drive in silence. I stared blankly at the road ahead, unaware of his constant talking. Mannerlessly, I had gotten down from his car and daze-walked to my home, unthankful for his gesture.

Nithin's dad peeked into my home daily thereafter. Neither did he ring the bell nor did he call out to me. He used to slip a note under an open window of my room. Sometimes he kept hot food outside the window and dropped a note through the window. Here was one person, who respected my privacy but at the same time, was concerned.

The first few days, the notes just read a simple text like, "Have a good day", "Rise as the sun shines", or "What is for lunch?"

I did not respond to any of them. He knew the notes were read though as the window stilt lay empty the next day, awaiting the pigeon post. I was getting used to this unusual visitor day-by-day. In fact, I looked forward to the notes. Once he knew I had surrendered to his meets, he started placing inspirational quotes. I used to sit on the bed, with the quotes and dissolved to each word of what it said. It kept replaying in my mind the entire day until the next one came. Only a few days later did I start putting sticky notes on the window, even if it read a simple "Thank you". My bedroom window was our postman. Our communication started through this medium.

Eventually, I opened up to him. I was caged between two worlds. In one of my detailed notes, I had mentioned to him that I was cowardly enough to take my life but not strong enough to lead a life too. I contemplated suicide N number of times. I did not have the "perfect plan" though. My sessions started from there on. I visited him quite often, not just on my sessions, but any other day when I felt like I needed a lending ear. Or even if it meant taking a hot lunch to him on some days. We met for miniscule chats sometimes at the same roadside tea stall from where he had picked me up first. Loneliness distanced from me. He was like a father to me, protecting me and being a friend at the same time.

My home was buzzing with colours again. The curtains had rolled up to welcome the sunshine in my life. Nights were more peaceful and dreamier. I came to terms with the death of my parents. If they would be proud, it will be because of how I survived rather than dying. Hence, I searched for a job again and when I was asked by interviewers on the long break I took, I proudly told the story of my survival from the dungeons of depression.

Hi again, I am Priya and that is my life, reborn as Version 2. Looks like death is not the only way to be reborn, life itself has opportunities to revive ourselves. Just need a hint of self-realisation.

Part Two

CHAPTER 16

Hope Stories

The guests swarmed out of the hall in flocks. I, Nithin, had personally begged the nine other Hope stories to stay back for a late-night party.

"Come on, Nithin! It is your wedding night! You ought to give yourself a rest. We could definitely catch-up some other time," joked one of them.

Well, I was serious though. They thought it was a joke.

"No,' I insisted. "I can't sleep without hearing your stories."

"And he won't let me sleep too," Priya added. "So you guys better stay."

All of them acknowledged my strange request at my own wedding. Nevertheless, they stayed back because they were just as curious to find out about the others as I was. The last of the guests were moving out. With a heavy sigh, Priya and I sat at the dinner table, with our special guests.

One of them asked me the first valid question.

"Why did you and Priya stand at extreme ends for a photo with us?" The young guy was too enthusiastic.

I had figured anyway that I would have started the conversation from that point. I answered like a detective.

"You see, when you started introducing yourselves to me, your names hid the puzzle I have been solving, or rather trying to solve. All I had, was dad's Hope files and in it were all of you. And each file signified the essence of your life. Eleven of us had won the game of life. Dad's Hope files, all of them, read only one thing that tied all of us together—our names."

"I still don't get the answer to why we were standing in a certain order for the photo," quipped a lady.

A smile came on my face. "Let us reveal our names in the same order and you will know for yourself as to why. Please remember the first letters of the sequence. Here it goes!"

At the extreme left is me.

Nithin - The bald guy. I shot my death.

Everest - The fat guy. I poisoned my death.

Vimal - The orphan. I jumped the hurdle of death.

Esha - The lost voice. I slit the throat of death.

Ruhi - The mother. I posted death on social media.

Gareema - The auto driver's daughter. I accidentally stumbled upon death.

Arvind - I am the usual love failure guy. I danced the death with fire.

Vishrutha - The dancing dream girl. I hung my death.

Evans - I am the memory loss case. I went missing with death.

Utkarsh - The injured sportsman. I drowned my death.

Priya - I am the dark-skinned girl. I suffocated death.

I shot one glance at everyone. All the others gasped. A few opened their mouths in wonder while others stared at each other with excitement. Priya and I were smiling at each other, contend to have accomplished a mission I had forcefully set out on.

Evans.

Evans spoke first. He dropped down in the chair, relaxed.

"Nithin, I am your dad's friend, he told me himself. We shared a close bond apparently. Once in two weeks he would meet me at the orphanage. He often took me to a park too and the same green bench. I had no idea why, but he said that was our meeting place. His sudden demise has come as a bit of a shock for me. I can still remember the days he met me at the orphanage." A tear trickled down his bouncy cheeks as he reminisced those days.

Vimal, who sat next to him, slid his palm on Uncle's palm and tried to calm him. I couldn't fathom why Vimal was already so touched by Evan uncle's story. He had just started. Vimal prompted Evans uncle to go on.

With a nod and leaving a big sigh, Evans uncle continued, "I was a mess. I could not remember one day to another. One hour to another. A part of my memory has still been washed away but he has brought in greenery to all the days he was with me. I now frequently visit my granddaughter, Charu. And if that meeting was possible, it is because of your dad."

"But I thought you went back home? Why an orphanage?" I asked. "Dad mentioned in his file that you only asked about Charu."

"Yes, I did. Because she was the only memory from my past that was glued to me. He never mentioned my past and neither did my son. But I am thankful to both for bringing Charu to my life again."

"That's nice. But why an orphanage? Why did you not go back home?" I urged.

"Your dad took me back to my home. I stood like a stone, just glaring at everybody," Evans replied sadly.

"Uncle, did you at least recognise Charu?"

"Probably dear. I remembered her name but her face was very vague in my mind."

I was ashamed at the little knowledge I possessed on his illness. So I changed the topic back to his stay in the orphanage.

"Uncle, it must have been good to know that you have a family and they must have been elated to have you back, right?" I asked the same question differently.

Uncle sighed again and dropped his shoulders and tried to remember. "I cannot remember their expressions, but my son hugged me. He was happy, I guess. Later, your dad told me that was because he could now get the property papers signed. I do not remember my home, my property, and neither did I intend to go back. Everything was strange. Everybody was a stranger. My son kept the papers on the table."

Uncle welled up again. This time, I wanted to comfort him. I did not want Vimal to get too emotional. This uncle was *my* father's friend.

I sat down beside his chair on the floor. Caressing his hand, I comforted him. "It's okay uncle. They were never yours."

Uncle brushed off my words, and he said, "No dear. It is not about them. Anyway, I hardly recognised them. It was just so hard with my condition that I had forgotten my signature too."

Well, I hadn't thought about that. As I proceeded back to my seat upon Priya's signal, feeling sad for Uncle Evans, Vimal consoles uncle again.

"How?" I thought in my mind. How is it that Uncle immediately becomes normal when Vimal calms him?

Meanwhile, Uncle proceeded, "Your dad told my son to bring an old signed document by me or an ink pad to take the signature as a fingerprint. My son promptly got an old document, I signed the papers that my son needed so desperately. Little did I know that it was a bargain. Your dad had made my son sign another paper in which it was written to allow Charu to meet me."

"Uncle, where do you live now?" One of the ladies questioned.

Finally! Someone else poked the question again. I was coming across as a very impatient person. Evans lifted his hands to touch a shoulder, sitting right beside him. Uncle smiled at last! Evans, pleased, looking straight into my eyes now and spoke.

"Nithin, please meet my adopted son, Vimal. And it is no more an orphanage! Ashraya Foundation is now a home for the elderly."

Instantly, my hand went to close my open, shocked mouth. Uncle now saw everyone and spoke again with great elation.

"Everyone, please see, this is my son. My son," he emphasised.

Everyone looked at each other, pleased and happy for them. Vimal stood and hugged his father tightly.

It was as though time had paused. We all wore a smile on our face as we watched them embrace each other and embrace the moment too. Vimal sat down after that long hug, smiling at us, now a tear trickling down his cheeks.

"We say we have one life, live it to the fullest, I say," said Evans uncle, almost as an ultimatum. "I got a new lease of life even in this life. And a better one too! I might have an illness that allows me this privilege, but anybody, at any point of time, can restart a life of their own. Restart in this lifetime itself. As a new you. As a you that you love."

Little did uncle know that he had set a context for the further stories to follow.

Vimal.

Here was a father-son duo, separated by bloodlines, coming together for a cause so touching. Evans uncle and Vimal now ran the orphanage that Vimal grew in. Vimal continued on from where uncle finished.

"Your dad had given me one piece of paper. In it, written in his cursive handwriting were the words—NEVER GIVE UP. In bold. And this was, by default, always with me. I was so obsessed with the craving for love of parents that I did not think of giving love rather than taking it. Isn't life all about give and take? I was blinded and it was my selfish nature. Also, how cowardly, right? It was at the height of the building when these thoughts had occurred. One more step, and I would have dropped dead."

Everyone gasped. This was the first time the flash of life's offerings hit everyone. I knew how this reaction felt as I knew all of their stories. This was the first when everyone started relating their stories too. *Oh boy! Welcome to the roller-coaster of emotions*. Here we go! Vimal let out a quick, hurried laugh as soon as he saw everyone's face.

"I felt the piece of paper in my pants pocket just when I rubbed off my sweaty hands on my pants," he continued. "Yes, I was scared. I was trying to gather strength. Once I had my mind sorted in those few moments, I climbed down, still in a trance. I was in a different world as I stepped down through the entire stairs. Once on ground, I looked up to the point where I had stood a while ago. I looked up at the point where my brains had left me."

A unison of laughter filled the room.

"You must have felt so stupid about that thought, right?" one of the guys asked.

"Absolutely!" Vimal threw his hands above. "I had decided that the next day, I will go to my therapist and hand over the piece of paper. I promised him that the paper was no longer needed. And that's how I survived!" Shame and pride were both on Vimal's face at the same time. "I am thankful to your dad, Nithin. If not for him, and for that small piece of paper, I would not be here to tell my story. I fully understood his questions to me, the answers he was trying for me to find out."

It was my turn for an emotional burst now; first of missing Pappa, and then came the realisation of the magnitude of impact his profession can bring.

"How did you find Evans uncle and how was he found by Nithin's dad?" The young guy probed.

"Just a few days after I had returned the paper to Nithin's dad, Papa had knocked on Ashraya," shared Vimal. "He seemed lost. All he wanted was a glass of water and something to eat. Seeing his deprived state, I rushed into the kitchen and provided him a plate full of rice and a big glass of water. I sat beside him on the small porch silently as he finished the meal in a jiff. Even as I was about to ask him any questions, he walked inside Ashraya, chose a room, and slept like a child.

I never let him go thereafter. A housemaid would tend to him while I was in office. I hardly cared who he was, where he came from. Papa did not recollect his name either."

"Then, what is his actual name? Is it not Evans?" asked a middle-aged man.

Vimal quickly laughed again. "His actual name *is* Evans. And I got to know this the first time Nithin's dad visited Ashraya."

"Nithin's dad never visited our houses! Why would he come to yours? Did you invite him?" The young guy angrily questioned. "As far as I know, he did not like personal visits."

"Young man, you got a temper as fit as mine! Of course, from my younger days," Vimal replied calmly. "I paid a visit once to Nithin's dad. Although I was glad that I found a father-figure, it also felt a bit uneasy to not know who he was. So I decided to consult Nithin's dad. Nithin's dad was a bit shocked to see me. He thought that the depression had gotten a hold of me again! When I explained him about Papa and that if he could come and see him, he had readily agreed due to Papa's age. Papa did not recognise him. But Nithin's dad's happiness knew no bounds. He told me that he was searching for Papa for many days and so were his family. That is when he started seeing him quite often at Ashraya. Papa may not evoke his earlier life fully, but he has definitely made my life a complete one. Papa still cannot remember one day to another. Nithin's dad told he was in stage two of Alzheimer's. There is as such no treatment prescribed. Nithin's dad only told me to take care of Papa and give him a life filled only with happiness for the remainder of his days. I am thankful to God for bestowing his care upon my shoulders. He can recollect a few memories of Charu and Nithin's dad. What Papa never forgets is to give me unconditional love each moment we spend together."

Evans uncle hugged Vimal and gave a little pat on his back. Vimal rubbed off the droplet of tear that came uninvited and continued.

"And yes, Ashraya is now a home for old people. Papa has been having a gala time with all the oldies around. There is only one rule imposed: nobody talks about their past. Time ticks ungenerously for them. You never know when death can knock on their soul. So, why live in a time when our own histories are bygones?" Vimal had made a point which everyone hibernated into.

Priya broke the silence. "Nithin's dad gave me that paper too! I too returned it to him. The paper was a constant reminder like a morning alarm to me. Once I was fully aware of the purpose of my life, I gave it back to him. That was the only favour I could finally return to him."

I held Priya's hand. "You are not the only one, my dear. We are in it."

Nithin and Priya.

Since Priya had already started our path, I continued to give out details.

"Evans uncle and I have something in common. Both of us never thought that we would be one of dad's files one day. Evans uncle and I never received that NEVER GIVE UP pledge, but our story was slowly building in his serene office. Both of us were closely related to him. When I was going through all our files, all that I had in my hands were your house addresses. Not a single name on it. My heart sank to see my own home's address on one of the files." I paused, just at the thought of reliving the files, most importantly my own. Priya pressed my hand to continue. "He was gathering details from me by questioning. He probed me a lot to speak out. I should have understood it. He was in that profession. But I went into a cocoon. Not letting Pappa into it, and not my friends either. I built a great-wall-of-Nithin around me."

Most of them chuckled.

"Depression seems like something that does not leave a therapist's son either," I said matter of factly. "I had my share of a depressed life, while I had a cloud of loving people around me. Priya came into my life just when I needed a companion who could understand my feelings. Being visibly under-developed in some areas of personified beauty, it made us close to each other and here we are today, being a man and a woman, as one soul. For all of us who have survived this game of devilish emotion, dad had taken back or you yourself had returned the NEVER GIVE UP papers. He made a smart correction in all your files. Instead of the 'I' in 'GIVE', he scratched it to an 'A'. All your files, now read as—

NEVER GIVE UP

A

Only for mine and Evans Uncle's files, he held the sheets himself and modified once he knew we would be sane again."

I turned towards Priya, suddenly perplexed,

"When did you return your NEVER GIVE UP chit?"

"Pappa never wanted you to find out about your file," Priya answered in a dull tone. "In one of our meetings, he spoke about you for a long time. Pappa, knowing both of us in and out now, knew that our ideologies matched a lot. So, he tried to match us! And voila, here we are today Nithin!"

I pressed her palms softly, promising enough to hold on tight for our lifetime. Priya continued talking.

"Nithin's dad had invited me to their house. The plan was to woo Nithin." She laughed hysterically and so did a few others. She continued with a glitter in her eye. "I liked Nithin's personality the moment I saw him. He fell for my intellect for sure. But he did not speak a word that day! Anyway, since the plan was to impress him, that was going smooth. Nithin's eyes were so fixated on me, that he did not pay heed to the happenings around him. Before I took leave of Pappa and Nithin, I had slipped the NEVER GIVE UP chit under the cup of coffee he had prepared for me." She came back to look at me now. She smiled. I sat open-mouthed. The love was brewing well.

Noticing everyone was uncomfortable in this atmosphere, I snapped out of the locked eyes on Priya.

"Alright! Alright! We do not plan to snatch the limelight!" I yelled. "Tonight, we want to hear you all. And we have so many more to go! I am sure, each of you would like to share your feelings." Like a proper host, I asked, "Who wants to go next?"

"I do," came a reply from one guy. And within a second, he also added, "I mean I want to go next to get the ice cream. It's pulling me to its magnetic charm. Do you guys mind?"

"I do," came a response from one lady, a bit harshly though.

"It's just one ice cream," he said and was already sprinting towards the ice-cream counter before the lady could say anything more. Her reaction was strange. Maybe she was impatient to sit and listen to others.

"Would you like to tell your story?" I offered. "I do not want to bother you for staying with us, if it's late."

"Oh no no. Please carry on. I didn't mean to interrupt like that," she said guiltily. "Let the ice cream guy come. I will speak later."

Now she wants to wait! Before I could assure her, Esha let herself in.

Esha.

Esha spoke next, flatly, reeling her memory quickly.

"You know, I debated with myself for a long time, not on the thought of dying, but the objective."

Everyone let out a small chuckle at her opening statement.

"Yeah, it sounds funny now. What is funnier is the very decision to give up on myself. I possess talent to reach out to people and inspire them by my words. Words are voices too. And people who do not want to hear my voice can read! Alas, what a waste of that period I was."

"All of us were, at one point," assured another lady.

Esha nodded and continued. "I had hung the NEVER GIVE UP paper just beside the photo of my family. On that fateful night, I gulped the nervous saliva and thrust it down my throat, ready for the knife to cut that breath. I would not be here today, sitting as an established writer if it were not for that one quick look at the family and the paper. Unfortunately, we live in a world of selfishness. And for once, that night, I thought about the people who loved me—my parents—and I lived for them! The zeal to dwell in their proud eyes overpowered the devil in me. And now, I can proudly tell, my voice is heard and inspiring people across the globe!"

The other lady in the room responded, "And I love your sweet voice too! And that is better than having harsh notes like mine."

Esha bowed. "Thank you. Yes, my voice is rare."

A quick flash of her file's end came to mind. "The file mentioned about the last poem you had written, which pretty much summed up your depression ordeal. Did that poem ever come out in the open?"

"That poem was never meant to be," Esha spoke with guilt. "It was titled *Unheard*. But yes, I never bothered to look at that poem. During one of those days of cleaning, my husband found it and we had a long discussion after that. A fruitful one though. I was in a happy space thereafter. After I returned the NEVER GIVE UP paper to your dad, that poem was burned too. The clarity of my life was clearer. My family supports and respects and is proud of me now!" She finished with each word stressing on the last sentence.

We all applauded her. So much said with such simplicity. She was a writer for a reason. Sharp and crisp with words.

"Esha, do you write poems?" Evans uncle asked. "I would love to read some in my home."

"Sure uncle! I would love to send across my poems," said Esha, elated. "Vimal, please pass on your house address. I will send you a book. It is a collation of my own poems. Uncle can read them."

"Is it available on Amazon?" Vimal enquired.

"Yes, it is. But I do receive author copies from my publisher. So I will just send them across."

"The greatest respect we can give to a writer is to buy the book," Evans uncle interjected. "Not by accepting it freely. We need to pay a price for her efforts."

"Esha, I will buy the book for Papa," Vimal chipped in. "Don't worry. Just give me the list of books."

Another man said, "I would love to read too." He turned towards another lady and said, "It could help us. Don't you think?" The lady nodded with enthusiasm.

And then there were a series of people asking for her books, except one. I wondered why one person supports another and the other does not. One does not want the other to eat ice cream. One wants to eat and others are okay with it. Weird people.

The ice-cream guy came back finally and snapped me out of the surroundings.

"I want them too!" he raised his hand.

"You mentioned you are an author. What are the books that you have written?" I asked Esha. "I must set myself on the reading path."

Esha reeled off her writing path for us. "I did start off with poems. They were the essence of my life. I suck in inspiration from around me. At a young age, it was nature, school, and teachers. As an adolescent it was about specific flowers, specific feelings, of studies, and of friends. As we stepped towards our twenties, I wrote about my parents, love, and relationships. Later, it turned into a darker side of things. As we progress in our relationships and life, we forget the child within us and responsibilities take over a mature us. When the child within me was leaving me, because society expects me to behave certain way, I lost myself too. My writings became more and more negative, with no fun, no creativity. My writings needed a new inspiration. I decided to write a biography as I love to know about others' lives, and choose someone who has been just like us. A story of overcoming obstacles."

Priya already knew, I guessed from her expression.

Esha laughed hard, and ended with a joke again. "I am glad I saved you from the trouble of reading the book. You could talk to the person directly and hear out his own survival story, in short. What say?"

"Wait, you are telling me that person is in this room?" I asked, puzzled.

Esha's eyes paved the road of our next victim of depression—

Utkarsh.

Utkarsh spoke with the utmost dignity, like a sportsman. "Esha's book titled, 'Strokes of Life', is an autobiography of my life. The book covers my entire life, from childhood to the day I challenged my being."

I was flabbergasted. If only I was a good book reader, I would have identified these famous personalities. Each one of us had lost a part of our life, relishing a hellish world, that we lost track of the beautiful things happening around us.

"I am a national-level swimming champion," Utkarsh continued. "And not many know of this because soon after the title win, I absconded from the competitions, from the media and from people too. I was not proud of that win."

"You should be proud of your every win and downfall, Utkarsh," Evans uncle comforted him. "Winning teaches us to be humble and losing teaches us lessons. Either way, we benefit. Why wouldn't you be proud?"

"Uncle, the competition for me, was not of my inbuilt talent but to compete with my own inner demons at that time. And I feel I did not handle that well. Knowing me well,

Nithin's dad had stuck the NEVER GIVE UP paper, just at the wall of my practice pool, in all four directions. The simple three words not only helped me but also everyone in the training camp. I would not have kept it personally anyway. He knew that. During practice, I never once saw that paper. Frankly, and not of any intention to hurt you Nithin, I thought your dad was crazy. I mean, who does this? Sticking papers under the swimming pool, outside, on the walls, even in changing rooms!"

That joke came a bit harsh on Pappa but Utkarsh was being honest here.

"But you still stuck to Pappa," I noted.

"I was comfortable talking to him only though," Utkarsh agreed. "His perspectives were different. And I understand them clearly now. He was patient with me and did not force anything for immediate action from my side. Only on that one day, when my mind, my nose, and my whole senses had switched off, the paper was clearly visible to get back my switch-on mode. I quickly pushed myself away from the downward pull of the water and breathed out, just like I pushed myself away from the stupidity I was going to commit. I gave the sheet of paper, four of them actually, back to your dad, also mentioning how his crazy idea had saved my life."

Everyone cracked up. Utkarsh continued as the laughter died down.

"I went into the nationals with a new me, and the new me had won the coveted title! Did I receive it with pride? No, my dear friend. This was not a win of my professional capability. It is lot more than the willingness to perform well."

Nobody dared to interrupt his talk, gobbling his high-level story, except of course, a shameless me.

"Utkarsh, what happened to your relationship with the bullies, afterwards?" I enquired.

"That day still feels like it went by in a hurry. I was in a hurry to set myself free. I was in a hurry to explore a version two of myself. I was in a hurry to practice and put the entire hundred percentage of not only my body but my mind as well. The day just rushed past, putting everything in the past. After giving back the papers to your dad, I came back and finally talked to everyone. I sat with them, and allowed them to dwell on the pain they had caused me. What surprised me is that they were shocked to hear that I was hurt. They said they joke around like this with many others too. Since the players are under pressure, a little loosening up is what they were looking for. But neither did they know that what might be a joke to them, maybe a part of bully rule to the receiver nor did they realise that I was slipping into depression because of it. Until I talked. That is what your dad always tried to tell me. You are feeding your depression because you are not vomiting the pain and letting others know. So it is not clearing your internals. You are just feeding."

Wow, what a dialogue, I thought.

"Did my dad say that?" I asked.

"Yes, he did!" Utkarsh confirmed. "The exact words. I wished then, if only I had vomited too, I would have felt better."

"Are you more socialising now or is this surrounding putting you in an uncomfortable position again?" I asked.

Utkarsh laughed. "I am fine now. I can handle people."

"What do you do now?" Priya questioned. "I have read Esha's book and it stops just where you also stopped now. And how did you meet Esha?" My love for Priya went a notch higher. At least one of us was an avid reader like my dad.

"As I already mentioned, I was looking for a good story to tell," Esha responded. "And I did not want to write just any story. I wanted to tell the world a real story. As you might already know, I loved newspapers and the journalism that came with it. That is when I stumbled upon the news about Utkarsh. One day, news came that he was a national-level winner. And a few days later it was followed by the news of his absconding. Well, he did not hide well though. He was housed in the same sports complex where he trained for the nationals."

She laughed thunderously.

"I had no intentions of hiding, by the way," Utkarsh cut in. "I just didn't want anybody in my life. But little did I know that this novice writer would come in search of me of all the people in the world!"

"Novice to an author now! Because of you!" Esha quipped. "But worth a story. He has had his struggles right from childhood. People had to be told that time can heal any wound. Only the duration of your patience matters."

All of us gave a nod.

"I am an instructor in the same institute where I did my training for the nationals," Utkarsh continued. "Only, I teach the underprivileged and those under nineteen years of age. My mantra is to give that which I didn't have back to society. I have been a part of many TEDx talks. Thanks to Esha's book, I got more publicity than I deserved. The goal is not to tell my story to inspire others, but to tell them that there is always a way out. To not only give yourself one more chance, but to also share the learnings of my life. If, in the audience, is at least one person who can go back home, be inspired, and stands to do something good to the society, my purpose of life is served."

Arvind and Vishrutha.

Just as Utkarsh was finishing his last sentence, Vishrutha laid out her part.

"Speaking of giving back to the society. That is what Arvind and I do. We run a dance-cum-theatre company that specialises in performances of meaningful life lessons. It is not just dance or acting for us. The story or the dance we build is always centred around societal misunderstandings or myths. This is also why we want to read Esha's poems and see if we can blend them into a dance of poetry."

Esha was happy to hear that. "Gladly! You could take whatever you like."

"We will make sure to give you due credits."

And then both, Esha and Vishrutha chuckled.

"But dad never mentioned about Arvind's dancing passion," I said, playing back their files in my mind.

"That was because dancing happened to me later," Arvind answered. "I did not mention it to him ever. The lady who saved me from the fire mishap is now my wife. We are happily married and are parents to two lovely kids."

"Oh! Love has found its way back to your heart!" I said joyfully and asked my next question. "I wonder, how did dance happen all of a sudden? Was Vishrutha your trainer?"

"Yes, Vishrutha was my trainer," said Arvind, nodding.

"But why dance to come out of your misery?"

"Nithin, when the fire was burning like hell, right in front of my face, I only saw her. She came running towards me and panting and puffing, she handed a paper to me, in which was written the exact words your dad had given me—NEVER GIVE UP."

My mind was definitely playing games that it wasn't designed to.

"Woah! Wait, are you telling me that your wife was my dad's Hope file too? Then, where is she? How did you meet Vishrutha then?"

While my questions were flying around indefinitely, Arvind and Vishrutha patiently waited until I had the answer myself. After a series of running thoughts, it hit me.

"Arvind, you and Vishrutha are married? She was the one who saved you?"

Arvind heaved a sigh. "Now you got it, my friend. Yes, she was the one who saved me. At least she was out of her suicidal thoughts when she met me. That night was the most beautiful night of my life. We talked for a long time, till dawn. The bride and groom were on their way to the mandap, at the exact point where I was supposed to give up on my life. From that day, I never stopped meeting Vishrutha. She let me into her world of dance. She had opened up a small studio with the cash prize she won."

"I see you have paved a way, just like your dance teacher," I mentioned to her after congratulating her. Vishrutha nodded happily.

"She mainly concentrated on teaching children," Arvind continued. "My training was an exception. And because of me, she commenced adults dance classes too! The pain healed as we talked about it openly. After every dance session, we talked endlessly till the young night fell on a not-so-young couple. I knew I had two ears which were always listening to me. And I had her back too. It helped us heal faster actually, since we shared our problems. Eventually, we had started to carve out a nice future for ourselves."

"This is a great love story!" said Vimal. "Worth another book for Esha!"

"Good catch, Vimal!" said Esha, elated. "I am already thinking of this."

"You are most welcome to, Esha," said Arvind. "Anything we can do to reach out to a larger audience, we are ready to do and be available for it. Not only as an inspiration to others, but also to tell our journey of opening a dance studio. Today, we run this company that gives us as much joy as the day when our pains had healed completely. The audience understands the problems of our society. We have performances to inject a completely different outlook towards life. Our performances based on children's mental health is a hit nowadays. We have so much more to offer and places to go with our concepts of addressing depression and mental health. It is taking shape and I am glad it is with the support of my loved ones."

Arvind then paved the way to his wife's story.

"Vishrutha, do you want to tell them what happened to the aerial act?"

"Yes!" said Vishrutha. "I was still staring at the payals that had fallen on the floor. Just give me one hint to not commit suicide, I was asking it. Often, the difference between living and not living is a fight between the heart and the mind. The mind plays games. The heart does not. My mind was telling to not live but if I was asking my payals to give me a chance, it meant, my heart told to live. I quickly untied the weapon of suicide. I got down the stool and ran to pick my payals. I placed it on my foot again. I had to win this competition. Whether my dad is proud or not, this win must be about me! This win must be about my survival! This win must be about my art! This win must be about breaking myths of girls dancing! This win must be to give courage to those who can, but, did not! And would my father be any prouder if I had committed suicide?"

She let the question linger around.

"Did you win?" I tried to change the topic.

"I did! I won!" She straightened her shoulders as she answered. She then raised her hands above her chest, proud of her accomplishment.

"What about your dad?" inquired Evans. "Did he come to terms with everything later?"

"He did not," Vishrutha replied, her shoulders slumping. "He still feels the same. I did not make him proud." She then spoke with elation. "But my mom did! She visits me often now. A restriction that has been lifted off by dad. She says she rebelled a lot to get that lift."

I suddenly remembered something.

"Vishrutha, in your file, it was never mentioned that you met my dad or took any sessions with him. I know of Arvind. But you? How did you receive that piece of paper?" I asked.

"Oh! I forgot to mention. Your dad was my greatest fan, I would say," answered Vishrutha. "He loved my performances during the competition. Just a few days before my final performance, your dad had come to the live audience meet. He had just handed over his visiting card to me, behind it were written the words, NEVER GIVE UP. He wished me luck for my future. Little did he or I know that we would meet one day. One of my payals fell. They slipped the same way, showing a path like when I left home, in the railway station. After unwelcoming a death ordeal, I visited your dad. That is when my therapy started. The sessions were going well. He gave me the actual NEVER GIVE UP slip then. Even though I had escaped death and won the life I wanted to live, I was not completely out of my mental state of mind when I met Arvind at that wedding. I was still peeling off my pain slowly."

"At times like these, moral and emotional support play a huge role. The power is even greater when the support is in the form of family and close friends," said one lady.

"True that, my friend!" Vishrutha agreed. "Mom had talked to me after the win. Dad, no. That is the reason I had not yet returned my paper to your dad. Like Arvind mentioned, it was when we started sharing our pain that it healed faster. We had both gone, together, to return our respective papers to your dad. I cannot explain how glad he was for us. We have always been indebted to him and his tiny idea of the paper, and we make sure these tiny things like food-for-thought, an object to make you wonder, or a good catch phrase, matter to all our performances. He has come for a few of our performances too. I still dance, my payals, surrendering to the power of healing through dance."

Evans uncle was like a kid, wanting everything he heard of. He turned towards Vimal and requested, "Can you take me to their dance show, next time?"

"Sure Papa," Vimal replied without hesitation. "We will go."

Vishrutha and Arvind extended their invitation to the others as well.

Everest.

The ice-cream guy, Everest, the youngest among our number, noted something that no one else could spot. "Did you guys notice the links within this room? Evans and Vimal, Nithin and Priya, Esha and Utkarsh, and Arvind and Vishrutha."

The room echoed with oh-yeses. As we looked to each other, seeing the connections, Everest questioned, "There is one catch though, which is that most of you know each other's lives! You know how the journey has been. But here I am taken aback to find one of my company's top executives wearing out her masked life. What are your bets, guys? Who could that be?" Ruhi and Gareema were the only two guesses.

"While you guys think, let me talk about my ordeal. As much as I love food, it was with great difficulty that I could train my mind and train my body too. I had no control over food, which is fine. What I needed was a way to burn them too. I was always under the impression that eating was bad because I was fat. But Nithin, your dad never called me that. He was making sure that losing weight was not going to be my main aim, as we usually think. Instead, being healthy is important. If that means, a loss of few kilograms, we should go towards that goal. He never ever made me feel like being a foodie is a bad thing. And that was the burning desire I reeled to when I saw the NEVER GIVE UP paper, right by the side of my food tray. I threw the poison to the far-right corner of my room, leading more rats to their death." He paused, looking angry.

Even with that face, this guy sounded funny. He was giving us a good laugh.

"Calm down," I said gently. "You should be happy to have gotten out of your cravings. But I do believe today you had a cheat day with ice-cream. Look at the art of your body now! How did you get to it?"

He laughed hysterically and continued talking, at the same time. "Oh man! This is hilarious. I never got out of my cravings."

"What do you mean? You still eat like before?" I asked, confused.

He stopped laughing. "Hell yeah man! Do come home sometime. My mom prepares delicious Parathas. Oh oh, that running butter, the escaping steam, and a tinkling pickle is all you need to escape a suicide."

Another roar of laughter. All our mouths were already open, and a few of us were already drooling over the Parathas in our head. Everest turned towards Evans Uncle.

"Uncle, please come home sometime. My mom would love to cook parathas for new guests." He already knew Evans uncle would ask for it anyway later, as he did for the others.

"Yes, sure dear," replied Evans Uncle gladly. "I will definitely come."

"Aren't we invited, Everest?" Utkarsh asked.

Everest, suddenly guilty, answered. "Oh, please do come. I am sorry, since uncle asked everyone else, I thought I should extend the invite to him. All of you are welcome at anytime!" Everest suddenly remembered something. "Hey guys! I should have mentioned this earlier. Along with my transformational journey, my mom also learnt different types of parathas. She made sure I never got bored of parathas and more importantly, I never need to quit eating my favourite food. So, she also started a small business initially. She would provide paratha lunch boxes for our apartment kids whenever the parents asked for it. She made a small amount of money from that. Slowly, she started as catering to small-sized parties. Everyone just loved her varieties."

"That is awesome, Everest!" Esha congratulated him. "There is no age limit to start anything new."

Everest thanked her and continued speaking.

"Absolutely agreed. My mother expanded her cooking, hiring women from the underprivileged sections, providing a livelihood to support their families too."

It was all so coincidental that everyone was doing their bit for the society. And to think of it, it is the same society who is also accountable for their pains. I was engrossed in these thoughts for a while, and I did not hear Everest calling me out.

Priya shook my hand and asked, "Are you okay?" I nodded and came to the present. Everest questioned me, apparently for the third time.

"Nithin, my mom now runs a small paratha joint near home. Can you guess what she named it?" He smirked.

I racked my brains to guess some name. Alas, I had to give up.

"Her joint is called—Parathas under the Pallu," Everest told with sparkling eyes. "Remember?"

I instantly knew what it meant and I provided context to the others.

"The gist of it is that Everest's safest places to tackle depression were parathas and tears under his mom's pallu. Aunty has used them both so wisely and creatively."

Everest agreed, "Yeah! It is actually cool. The place is covered with saree pallus on the ceilings."

"That sounds like a culturist interior. We would love to visit," said Arvind. "Do you have the urge to walk-in and eat, considering you have to maintain a certain level of fitness?"

"Yes, I never controlled my eating and nor do I now," Everest continued seriously. "I figured, well, that I need a figure. I did not stop at jogging in the morning. I went to the gym daily. I got into sports, badminton, mainly. I started caring for my body like never before. But what I did with my food was nobody's business. I made sure I got it out of the system. I could feel the change in me. Now that I got the abs and the swag, I like to show off, you see. So, I started applying for modelling jobs. The day I signed the contract with…" He paused abruptly.

We eagerly waited for him to continue. He prompted us to think more. Oh, this was the cue where we should be guessing the other linked person in the room. He did not wait for any of our response. We took too long to come up with the name. He unveiled, marking each of his word with a slow pause.

"The day I signed the contract with the harshest voice in this room, I handed the NEVER GIVE UP slip back to your dad! Oh boy, wasn't he happy? He hugged me tight, and for the first time, he could feel his entire hand perfectly wrapping around me without the distraction of my belly."

We all roared with laughter this time.

Gareema.

"Yes, that is a bit surprising to see one of my top male models here tonight, who has lived through a period of depression, just like me."

Oh, this was the same lady who had asked Everest not to go towards the ice-cream counter.

"Is that why you stopped him from eating ice-cream? Because models are following any diet?" I questioned her, now that we knew he was a model. "I thought they were entitled for a cheat-day."

I winked at Everest, who winked back at me.

Gareema, very composed, replied, "At our company, we do not differentiate models by sizes, age, gender, or caste. Instead, we are very particular of their behaviour on the shoots, or on ramp walks. We, as a company, respect models, irrespective of their background and we expect the same respect for all the company employees, at whatever level they be. So, I just felt like Everest disrespected our conversations by getting up abruptly."

Vimal brushed it off, saying, "None of us felt that way. Chill."

Gareema heaved a sigh of relief.

"See! I upheld our company's reputation," Everest teased her. She gave a smile to which Everest roared again with laughter.

Gareema then started her story.

"I am not used to talking much, so I will keep my story short. So, as you know, Nithin, I tried to end my life, at the same time thinking of not making it look like a suicide. I did not want to bring any shame to my family. I just sat on the road, my eyes empty. The lights of the truck had flashed on my eyes, just at the same time the famous NEVER GIVE UP slogan had flashed in front of my eyes. The distant auto sound sparked the fluorescent colour of the words. It was dad. My eyes suddenly filled with embarrassment. For once, I was thankful to your dad and also my dad. Your dad knew that to heal my pain, he had to serve me with the same dish. The faster I ate it, the faster I would realise its taste. Everything was a part of life and he needed me to gobble that part up. I would not cooperate for even one session. My inner debates were bursting at him. He knew my weakness though: my dad. So, he had got the words painted in shining bold on the front of my dad's auto. And he kept repeating those words in every session. And he made me shout it loud every time I ran towards the door of his office. With that super-colourful flash of my dad's auto and the words of NEVER GIVE UP, I quickly swerved to the left, hitting a small rock. Pockets of blood blasted. I did not feel the pain as I knew this was not my real pain."

"And all I wanted was validation from my father," said Vishrutha. "You are lucky, Gareema. Your father has stood by you in difficult times."

"Isn't that also the age when we stumble more and look for a hand to pick us up? My dad's hand were always extended towards me," Gareema acknowledged. "All my life had been a struggle until then. My parents had suffered way longer than I had though. And they have pulled along, for my sake, working hard daily, to give me a good education. There, I stood, dead in the night, not willing to even give a small percentage of my share towards working hard. My parents lived for me, no matter what was thrown to them by life. It was my time to give a lot more to them. My mind was so blocked, due to my status, my background, and more that I needed a small piece of sympathy from someone to unblock it. Only that made me happy. I am poor, I gotta be given sympathy, was my mantra. I had everything in my hands, a loving family and a deserving education, and I was cribbing of the silliest things of life. Just because I was born poor. I decided I am not going to let that be."

Gareema paused. Even though she came across as a tough lady on the outside, she was tearing up inside. She started crying profusely. All the ladies rushed towards where she was seated. They started calming her, as all of us boys sat, head bent down. Everest slowly walked to her and comforted her too.

"You are strong. Stay put," he said gently. "We are all with you." As Gareema's tears gradually reduced, Everest asked, "You made me tense, can I get another ice-cream?" Gareema's tears flew away and she burst into a laughter, as did everyone else.

Such a funny guy, but also a good-to-have friend at such times. A friend who can crack you up instead of sympathising. Ironically, the only thing that Gareema was looking for in a somewhere previous life of hers.

Gareema rubbed her eyes dry like a child and continued as though nothing happened. "All I had to do was bank on my knowledge and an ATM to withdraw it every day. I have grown in this modelling agency like nobody else. I am *not* one of the top executives of the company. I am the company. I founded this company with all my heart. I needed a place to start afresh. Today, if there is anything I can be thankful for, it is that anthem of NEVER GIVE UP. Your dad did make sure all of us tattooed it in our mind, permanently, seems like."

"Now, it makes sense to me," said Everest, his thoughts leaking out.

"What does?" I asked.

Everest had to end it his way. "This lady, my boss, every day comes to office in an auto and it is the same guy every day! That too an older one! That is your dad, right?"

Gareema nodded in agreement.

Everest laughed at his own jokes. "Hahaha, you know there's a love angle link-up between you two doing the rounds in office, right?"

Gareema, being the boss lady, asked, "I wouldn't mind replacing him with a younger driver. Maybe you?" She hung the joke in the air with a wink.

Ruhi.

Everest was the most restless amongst us all, not only physically, but mentally as well. As we had progressed through each of our journeys, he was taking my place; that of being inquisitive. His mind was on a marathon spree, faster than our minds could catch up. All of us steadily sunk each of our stories while Everest had already begun spinning a new theory.

Everest, speaking hurriedly, "Guys guys, we are eleven. And ten of us have already had our links set up. Basically, we are five pairs of Hopes."

He slowly turns towards Ruhi, as we all did. He read our minds, and asks her the obvious question.

"You are the only one left. Without a string attached to any of us. What is your story, the un-linked one?"

Ruhi smiled and began to tell her story. "Every mother, in general, fails to acknowledge herself as strong. Actually, the word 'Mother' itself is a synonym to strength. As a new mother, I failed to self-please. The initial days of attending to my child was tiring, physically and, I was not made to do household chores a lot. Suddenly, I lived in a free world. While my child slept, I could do anything. A young me, rather, chose to be on the social media. Instagram, Facebook, Twitter—I was there! I was a silent spectator, more of a spy I would say."

"It is a scary place but good for publicity for companies like ours," said Everest. "Being a show-off myself, I keep posting. The attention is nice."

"I am not so active on social media but Priya is. She found this venue through her suggestions in Instagram. I like the positives of it," I said, seconding his thoughts.

"That's the whole point!" Ruhi argued. "See, we now have Priya who rightly got something good for her. Whereas Everest, people follow him for the profession he is in and get inspired too. Think about this though. Did any of those followers know of his depression, unless he posts about it? That is a life he needs to frame on social media too."

Gareema came to Everest's rescue. "He did post. A long story of his depression. He gained more followers thereafter."

"That's a brave move, Everest," Ruhi said, lauding him. "Unfortunately, many do not. They lead a dual life. One for people to see. Another is the reality they do not show. Just out of a pregnancy, my physical being was undergoing changes. To watch my friends and relatives leading a happy life was not a comfortable space. But I liked to see their posts, their photos. Just to envy more. Cold shoulders from my family too made me feel sick inside."

I spoke to her before she could cry. "How did you overcome it, Ruhi? What was the turning point?"

"Once I started spending more time with my growing daughter, social media did not bother me," Ruhi answered. "I realised that people were faking a lot of things to the world while their own world was stumbling. A photo of a couple in Maldives does not describe their day-to-day life. A parent wishing their own kid on Facebook while the kid is yearning for your face time is not parenting. Showing off a graduation certificate to the universe is not as cool as calling up that one friend who is happy to see that photo. But, publishing a sad self, of how bad a cook you were or just posting your kid's tantrums with you, is the true you. Stop for a while when you browse anything on social media and think, was it okay to be jealous of the couple, was I happy for my friend's educational qualifications, was I being judgmental of the cuteness of somebody else's baby rather than cuddling my own, was I being myself in front of the world?

My daughter was a toddler when it stuck to me. I had to live for her. We mothers, unfortunately, are constantly trying to be the best we could be. We often fail though. Because we do not realise that each mother is the best for their child. I had to get my head straightened out. What example can I set for my daughter? Later in her life, she should be as proud of me as I will be of her. Her upbringing depends on my wellbeing. That is when I decided to stop this foolishness. I locked up my phone for the whole day. At night, I would check my messages. For a few days, it was difficult as the temptation of social media tried to lure me towards it. But my daughter's love, pranks, and playfulness did the tricks to lure me away from social-*keeda*. Oops, sorry, social media. But, really, they are the same."

We laughed at her accidental joke. But I had more questions.

"Being social is the way of life now. It is a love-hate relationship, right?" I asked. "So, are you telling me that you have no presence on any of the social-media platforms?"

She shook her head. "No! I am all over the place now. Facebook, Instagram, and Twitter are the sides of my dish. The main one is my own website where I serve the best dishes. I would never advise anyone to stop using these platforms. They are great, but only if utilised in the right way. Initially, I was venting out a lot of sadness. When people sympathised with comments, it felt better. After a while, even they got tired of my constant nagging. Youngsters need words that they can relate to, and about telling them to deal with it. What does not go out of style and praising from others is if you give them a good laugh out of something serious that happened in your life, but also how did you take the positive out of it. You can get them to read some inspiring quotes or write one of your own! And that is what I serve my followers now. A good quote on life, every now and then. And let me tell you, that never does a thumbs down! So, yes, for your question, I am active on social media, for relevant purposes. My first positive short story was liked by Nithin's dad, and I remember him sharing it on his social media handles too! It really is all about the perspective."

Everest hummed and asked again. "You sound more and more like Nithin's dad. So then, you are still not linked to anyone, right?"

Ruhi concluded with a smile, "You answered it already!"

CHAPTER 17

The Office: Part Two

Priya and I had gotten the office dusted and cleaned. We retired the old office, and gave it a fresh new look. The interiors were bright now. Just as we were arranging a flower-vase, the new owner of this office stepped in. We greeted her warmly, with a bouquet of flowers. She came with her daughter. We gave her a few minutes to sink in the room, her office from today.

We wished her the best of luck. I was about to take the photo of my family, up from the table but Ruhi sat on the chair and stopped my hand from lifting the photo frame.

"He will always belong and inspire me here," Ruhi assured me. My eyes thanked her, words failing to come out. Ruhi's daughter carefully placed her family photo beside ours.

"Now you know my link," Ruhi continued. "It was your dad!"

I was not convinced. "When you are already inspiring people on social media, why therapy?"

"Not all people are social-keeda," she said seriously. "There are a lot of them out there who can get inspired by words but would not know what to do next. I have had people pinging me after reading my stuff about how it has helped them, and what they did to overcome their struggle in life. Not all of them are like that. Some need a face-to-face conversation, to give them quality time and allow them to vent out anything in this world. Over time, I came to love this part. The part of being there for someone and provide solace. The part of making a difference in others' lives. The part where I can understand a person's feeling because I went through some part of it. The part of knowing that there is so much hate in the world and yet to teach others of loving oneself. The part of drowning into somebody else's story and making it a damn good one for them. I did not know where to start though, and for that, I must thank your dad for supporting me. You know, he would always say that I was thinking and seeing everything in the wrong way. I had grasped the meaning of it later. We see others' lives just the way they show it. Who knows what torments their lives from inside the walls of their home or even for that matter, their inner well-being? Have they been true to the real world? Have I been the mother a daughter wants to be in the future? With that notion, I deleted my suicide posts soon after and returned the NEVER GIVE UP slip to your dad. I trained under him for a while and then he suggested me to take appropriate courses and get a certified therapist label."

* * *

My dad had poked Ruhi's mind.

"Your mind is always wandering, thinking of others, which is good," he had said. "But you are thinking in the wrong way. You have an urge to read people's mind, give solace to the wounded ones. But you have been reading them all wrong. Why don't you consider studying therapy? Nothing stops you from relearning your past and starting a new chapter."

"But, I am a mother, growing older, I have a family to take care of," Ruhi had objected.

"Don't do the math at your age, do the math on your heart's age. What does it say? And dear, if you cannot convince your family of your plans, how will you convince the world? Get your family onboard with your future plans. And being a mother? A mother knows no bounds, in whatsoever she does. She can be a super-woman and a sensitive woman, all at the same time. You have the natural knack for being strong and caring for multiple people at the same time. You can do this!"

Ruhi said that with these heavy-lifting words, she had lifted her life, picked it up from the pieces she had strewn around till now. A few talents picked up from her childhood, the enthusiasm she had forgotten in her youth, and the financial needs in her adulthood. Armed with the vessels of her family's support and her zeal to be alive for her daughter, she had cooked up a great educational journey.

Pappa had offered Ruhi good books to read on being a therapist first. Then, a full-fledged course. At first, she was vehement. Am I right for this job? I am a mother; how could I give my time to other things? Is it too late of an age to pursue a career? Questions, questions, and only questions.

Pappa had signed-off with the last of his words that she can remember: "the dictionary of a mother does not admit the word 'Impossible'."

Ruhi was looking for a serene space to establish her office, one that did not look like a mental asylum. That is when my invitation had knocked on her door. She knew exactly the place to reap the fruits of her knowledge.

Priya and I closed the door behind us, allowing Ruhi to open her door to inspire and heal others.

For the last time, the wind blew on my face, a cooler one. Finally, he had reached his attainment, my Pappa. I glanced at what looked like a sun-kissed cloud.

"Yes dad, I will NEVER GIVE UP," I shouted through the waving clouds.

Remember the cake? Whole-heartedly eaten and fully contented.

My heart felt much lighter, as the rains poured to quench my tears.

Acknowledgments

I would like to take a moment to express gratitude to everyone who embarked on this journey with me.

To my parents, Mr. G R Guruprasad and Mrs. Bhagyalakshmi for their unwavering support. Thank you for being an inspiration to me.

To my family and friends, who have stood by my side and encouraged me throughout—a heartfelt thank you.

Then, to the Nu Voice Press team—Abhishek, Vini, Vedika, Navya, Arya, Archita, and everybody else. You have owned each word and emotion of the book as much as I have, or probably even more. Thank you for all the hard work in making *Never Give Up*.

Finally, to this life.

About the Author

Divya G Prasad finds her roots in Bengaluru, India. While she is an IT professional, her heart pulls her back to her passion—writing.

Divya's poems have found their way into international and national anthologies, starting from 9th class onwards. Her poems range from a spectrum of emotions throughout her growing years. Divya strongly believes in taking inspiration from those around her—families and friends.

Divya sticks by her rule of writing; keep it simple, but twisted, yet different.